TENNIS

Steps to Success

Jim Brown, PhD
McNeese University
Lake Charles, Louisiana

Leisure Press
Champaign, Illinois

Library of Congress Cataloging-in-Publication Data

Brown, Jim, 1940-
  Tennis: steps to success / Jim Brown.
    p. cm.—(Steps to success activity series)
  ISBN 0-88011-318-9
  1. Tennis.   I. Title.   II. Series.
GV995.B6924 1989
796.342'2—dc19   88-2458

Developmental Editor: Judy Patterson Wright, PhD
Production Director: Ernie Noa
Copy Editor: Peter Nelson
Assistant Editors: Kathy Kane and Robert King
Proofreader: Laurie McGee
Typesetter: Yvonne Winsor
Text Design: Keith Blomberg
Text Layout: Tara Welsch
Cover Design: Jack Davis
Cover Photo: Bill Morrow
Illustrations By: Raneé Rogers and Gretchen Walters
Printed By: United Graphics, Inc.

Instructional Designer for the Steps to Success Activity Series: Joan N. Vickers, EdD

ISBN: 0-88011-318-9

Printed in the United States of America

10 9 8 7 6 5

Leisure Press
A Division of Human Kinetics Publishers, Inc.
Box 5076, Champaign, IL 61825-5076
1-800-747-4457

UK Office:
Human Kinetics Publishers (UK) Ltd.
PO Box 18
Rawdon, Leeds LS19 6TG
England
(0532) 504211

Canada Office:
Human Kinetics Publishers, Inc.
P.O. Box 2503, Windsor, ON N8Y 4S2
1-800-465-7301 (in Canada only)

Contents

Series Preface

The Steps to Success Activity Series is a breakthrough in skill instruction through the development of complete learning progressions—the *steps to success*. These *steps* help students quickly perform basic skills successfully and prepare them to acquire advanced skills readily. At each step, students are encouraged to learn at their own pace and to integrate their new skills into the total action of the activity, which motivates them to achieve.

The unique features of the Steps to Success Activity Series are the result of comprehensive development—through analyzing existing activity books, incorporating the latest research from the sport sciences and consulting with students, instructors, teacher educators, and administrators. This groundwork pointed up the need for three different types of books—for participants, instructors, and teacher educators—which we have created and together comprise the Steps to Success Activity Series.

The *participant book* for each activity is a self-paced, step-by-step guide; learners can use it as a primary resource for a beginning activity class or as a self-instructional guide. The unique features of each *step* in the participant book include

- sequential illustrations that clearly show proper technique for all basic skills,
- helpful suggestions for detecting and correcting errors,
- excellent drill progressions with accompanying *Success Goals* for measuring performance, and
- a complete checklist for each basic skill for a trained observer to rate the learner's technique.

A comprehensive *instructor guide* accompanies the participant's book for each activity, emphasizing how to individualize instruction. Each *step* of the instructor's guide promotes successful teaching and learning with

- teaching cues (*Keys to Success*) that emphasize fluidity, rhythm, and wholeness,

- criterion-referenced rating charts for evaluating a participant's initial skill level,
- suggestions for observing and correcting typical errors,
- tips for group management and safety,
- ideas for adapting every drill to increase or decrease the difficulty level,
- quantitative evaluations for all drills (*Success Goals*), and
- a complete test bank of written questions.

The series textbook, *Instructional Design for Teaching Physical Activities*, explains the *steps to success* model, which is the basis for the Steps to Success Activity Series. Teacher educators can use this text in their professional preparation classes to help future teachers and coaches learn how to design effective physical activity programs in school, recreation, or community teaching and coaching settings.

After identifying the need for participant, instructor, and teacher educator texts, we refined the *steps to success* instructional design model and developed prototypes for the participant and the instructor books. Once these prototypes were fine-tuned, we carefully selected authors for the activities who were not only thoroughly familiar with their sports but had years of experience in teaching them. Each author had to be known as a gifted instructor who understands the teaching of sport so thoroughly that he or she could readily apply the *steps to success* model.

Next, all of the participant and instructor manuscripts were carefully developed to meet the guidelines of the *steps to success* model. Then our production team, along with outstanding artists, created a highly visual, user-friendly series of books.

The result: The Steps to Success Activity Series is the premier sports instructional series available today. The participant books are the best available for helping you to become a master player, the instructor guides will help you to become a master teacher, and the teacher educator's text prepares you to design your own programs.

This series would not have been possible without the contributions of the following:

- Dr. Joan Vickers, instructional design expert,
- Dr. Rainer Martens, Publisher,
- the staff of Human Kinetics Publishers, and
- the *many* students, teachers, coaches, consultants, teacher educators, specialists, and administrators who shared their ideas—and dreams.

Judy Patterson Wright
Series Editor

This book is three books in one. First, it is a book for players enrolled in tennis classes offered through colleges, high schools, clubs, and municipal programs. It will take you step-by-step through the process of learning how to play and enjoy tennis. In this case, the term step-by-step is not just a figure of speech. The series of instructional steps are specifically designed so that each step prepares you for the next one. These steps are based on my experience as a player, instructor, coach, teaching professional, and tennis clinician. They were not invented just for this book. Every person I teach goes through this progression—individuals may progress at different rates, but they all take each step along the way.

This is also a book for people who have played some tennis before. No one ever becomes a perfect player. All of us keep trying to refine our shots, develop new ones, use strategy more effectively, and move up to better competition. *Tennis: Steps to Success* can help you analyze your game and make changes where they are needed. The detail on fundamentals and strategy will allow you to evaluate what you are doing on the court. Using this book you can establish new patterns, change old ones, and improve on what you are already doing.

Finally, this book is written for those who may have no access to tennis classes. Some people, including me, learned to play tennis without taking lessons. By reading, observing, imitating others, asking questions, and most of all, practicing and playing, you may be able to learn on your own, too. It is not the best method, but it can be done. Consider *Tennis: Steps to Success* as a manual for teaching yourself the game. Follow each step, adding your own talent and personality to the fundamentals—the "Keys to Success"—presented. If you can eventually get some instruction, that will be a bonus.

Writing this book has given me the opportunity to examine and record my own style of playing and teaching tennis. The game has changed dramatically in the past 20 years, and the methods of teaching others to play it have changed, also. By writing both this book and the instructor's manual (*Teaching Tennis: Steps to Success*) at the same time, I have been able to ensure that you, the student, and the person teaching you are figuratively and literally on the same page in the instructional process. I know you will want to move through the steps to becoming a good tennis player as quickly as possible. In going through the steps myself from the perspective of both player and instructor, I have tried to make the process not just faster, but enjoyable as well.

I want to thank Human Kinetics Publishers for the opportunity to share my tennis experiences with others. I also want to thank the players of southwest Louisiana for providing a living laboratory for my tennis theories and methods. And finally, thanks to Arlene and Matthew Brown for listening to ideas, reading copy, questioning methods, posing for pictures, giving up computer time, and supporting my work as a teacher and writer.

Jim Brown

The Steps to Success Staircase

Get ready to climb a staircase—one that will lead you to be a great tennis player. You cannot leap to the top; you get there by climbing one step at a time.

Each of the 19 steps you will take is an easy transition from the one before. The first few steps of the staircase provide a foundation—a solid foundation of basic skills and concepts. As you progress further, you will learn how to connect groups of those seemingly isolated skills. Practicing common combinations of tennis skills will give you the experience you need to begin making natural and accurate decisions on the tennis court. You will learn to choose the proper stroke to match your various tennis needs—whether for quickness, power, deception, or just fun. As you near the top of the staircase, the climb will ease, and you'll find that you have developed a sense of confidence in your tennis abilities that makes further progress a real joy.

To prepare to become a good climber, familiarize yourself with this section as well as "The Game of Tennis," "Tennis Equipment" and the "Warming Up for Success" sections for an orientation and in order to understand how to set up your practice sessions around the steps.

Follow the same sequence each step of the way:

1. Read the explanations of what is covered in the step, why the step is important, and how to execute or perform the step's focus, which may be a basic skill, concept, or tactic, or combination of the three.
2. Follow the numbered illustrations showing exactly how to position your body to execute each basic skill successfully. There are three general parts to each skill: preparation (getting into a starting position), execution (performing the skill that is the focus of the step), and follow-through (recovering to starting position). These are your "Keys to Success."
3. Look over the descriptions of common errors that may occur and the recommendations for how to correct them.
4. Read the directions and the Success Goal for each drill. Practice accordingly, record your score, and compare your score with the Success Goal. You need to meet the Success Goal of each drill before moving on to practice the next one, because the drills are arranged in an easy-to-difficult progression. This sequence is designed specifically to help you achieve continual success. The drills help you improve your skills through repetition and purposeful practice.
5. As soon as you can reach all the Success Goals for one step, you are ready for a qualified observer—such as your teacher, coach, pro, or trained partner—to evaluate your basic skill technique with the Keys to Success Checklist. This is a qualitative, or subjective, evaluation of your basic technique or form—and using correct form can enhance your performance. Your evaluator can tailor specific goals for you, if they are needed, by using the Individual Program form (see Appendix).
6. Go through these procedures for each of the 19 Steps to Success. Then rate yourself according to the directions for "Rating Your Total Progress."

Good luck on your step-by-step journey to developing your tennis skills, building confidence, experiencing success, and having fun!

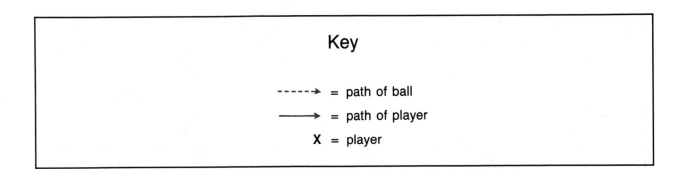

The Game of Tennis

When Walter Wingfield received a British patent for lawn tennis in 1874, he could not have predicted what the game would be like today. Tennis, perhaps more than any sport, has changed drastically in a relatively short period of time.

Not long ago, tennis was a game played mostly by rich men who belonged to exclusive clubs. Although club tennis is still strong, people of all socioeconomic classes now play, and in the United States, most play on public courts. When the United States Lawn Tennis Association (now the United States Tennis Association) extended its "protective wing" to women in 1889, tennis became a respectable, if not popular, sport for both sexes. By the mid-1970s, as many women were playing as men.

Players now range in age from the 8-and-under group to the over-70 division. Surveys indicate that between 10 and 15 million Americans play tennis regularly. Most are amateurs who play for fun with friends, in tournaments, on teams, and in leagues throughout the country.

TENNIS TODAY

Once tennis was played only by amateurs. Now world-class players often turn professional during their teens and early twenties. Open tennis, in which professionals can compete with amateurs, was a development of the 1960s, and tennis remains one of the few sports in which this happens regularly.

More than any other factor, television has been responsible for the changes in tennis. The increase in the number of players, products, and programs happened almost simultaneously with the increase in tennis events shown on television. Now major events like Wimbledon (played in England) and the U.S. Open attract audiences of millions around the world.

Tennis has also been changed by technology. Once courts were made only of grass, clay, or concrete. Now they are also made of colorful synthetic products with made-to-order surfaces. Tennis rackets have gone from wood to space-age products like graphite, boron, ceramics, fiberglass, and Kevlar. The size of racket heads ranges from the traditional 60–80 square inches to jumbo sizes of 116 inches and more.

Finally, tennis instruction has changed. During the first two thirds of the century, there was not enough interest to support many teaching professionals. Now there are tennis pros, teachers, coaches, camps, courses, and clinics throughout the country. There are also organizations and businesses that train and certify people to become professionals.

If you are interested in becoming more involved in the game, join the United States Tennis Association, 1212 Avenue of the Americas, New York, NY 10036. Its members can play in sponsored tournaments, receive tennis publications, improve by getting professional instruction, and obtain other benefits of belonging to an organization with hundreds of thousands of members interested in the game.

PLAYING A GAME

Singles is a match between two players. *Doubles* is a match between four players—two on each team. *Mixed doubles* is a match pairing a man and woman on one team against a man and woman on the other team.

After a brief warm-up, the players decide by spinning a racket or flipping a coin who will serve first and on which ends of the court they will begin the match. The ball is put into play by a *serve*, and the *point* is played out. Points are won by forcing the opponent to hit into the net, hit outside of the boundary lines, or not hit the ball before it bounces twice. After the serve, players may hit the ball before or after it has bounced on the court.

One player serves an entire *game*, which may last as few as 4 points or as many as an indefinite number of points. The *server* alternately serves from the right and left sides of the center mark to the *receiver*, who also moves back and forth from right to left to return the serve. A *set* is won when one player has won at least 6 games and is ahead by at least 2 games. The final score in a set might be 6-0, 6-1, 6-2, 6-3, 6-4, 7-5, 8-6, or so on.

A player wins a *match* by winning 2 out of 3, or 3 out of 5, sets. When time is limited, pro sets might constitute a match. A *pro set* is won by the player who wins at least 8 games and who is ahead by at least 2 games. Players exchange ends of the court when the total number of games played in a set is an odd number.

In most matches, players are responsible for keeping their own scores and for calling shots "in" or "out." No sound from a player means the shot is *in* (inbounds), and play continues. Shots that hit the lines are good. *Out* means the ball landed outside the boundary line, and the point is over. In some tournament competition, an *umpire* may stand or sit near the net, call out the score, and settle disputes on close shots. At higher levels of the game, *linespersons* are positioned to make line calls. See Figure 1 to learn the lines and areas of the court.

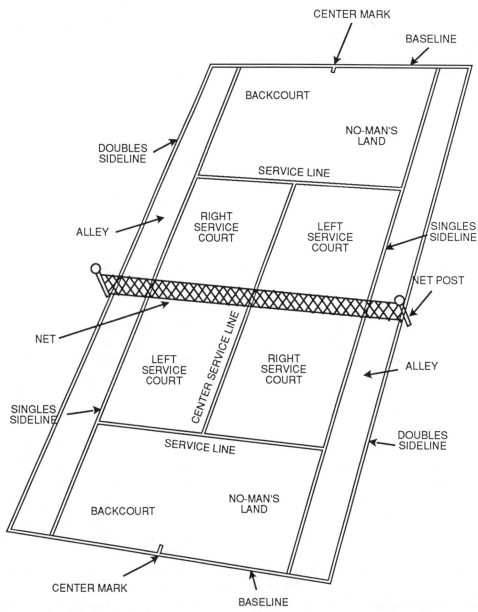

Figure 1 Court lines and areas.

Singles Rules

Singles players take all practice shots before the match begins. Warm-ups are usually limited to 5 minutes. Before the match begins, the player who wins the racket spin or coin toss may choose whether to serve or receive, or to play the first game on the side of his or her choice. The other player gets to choose whatever is left—serve or receive, or side of court.

The server stands behind the baseline, to the right of the extended *center mark* and inside of the *singles sideline* to the right as he or she faces the net for the first point. When the opponent is ready, the server has two chances to put the ball into play by tossing and hitting it into the *service court* across the net diagonally from the serving position on the baseline. The receiver is ready if he or she attempts to return the serve. The server cannot step on or beyond the baseline before striking the ball. The receiver can stand anywhere, but must let the ball bounce after the serve before returning it. After each point, the server lines up on the other side of the center mark to begin the next point. If a ball hits the top of the net and goes into the proper court, that serve is called a *let*. The serve is repeated without the let counting against the allotted two attempts.

In summary, you can win points if your opponent

- fails in both attempts to serve the ball into the proper court,
- hits the ball outside of the proper boundary lines,
- hits the ball into the net,
- lets the ball bounce twice before returning it,
- reaches over the net to hit a ball before it has bounced,
- throws the racket and hits the ball,
- touches the net with the body or racket while the ball is in play,
- deliberately carries or catches the ball on the racket strings,
- does anything to hinder the opponent in making a shot,
- touches the ball with anything other than the racket during a point, or
- touches or catches the ball during a point, even if standing outside the court.

Doubles Rules

The doubles server may stand anywhere behind the baseline between the center mark and the *doubles sideline*. Players on each team take turns serving entire games. The order of serving stays the same throughout the set. Receivers decide who will receive serves on the right and left sides, respectively, and maintain that order throughout the set. Other rules described for singles apply to doubles, except that after the serve, the areas between the singles and doubles sidelines (*alleys*) are in play (see Figure 1).

SCORING

The server's score is always given first. Points are *love* (0), *15* (the first point won by either player), *30* (the second point), *40* (the third point), and *game* (fourth point). If the players are tied at 3 or more points during a game, the score is called *deuce*. When the server goes ahead by 1 point after the score was deuce, the score is *ad in* or *advantage server*; if the receiver is ahead, it's *ad out*. A player must win 2 consecutive points after the score was deuce in order to win that game. If not, the score goes back to deuce.

No-Ad Scoring

No-ad scoring was introduced in the 1970s to simplify keeping score and to reduce the length of matches. It is much easier for casual fans and even for players to learn and remember the simple 1-2-3 no-ad system than the 15-30-40-deuce-ad method. Because no-ad scoring eliminates the requirement of having to win games by at least 2 points, the overall length of tennis matches can be reduced considerably. High school and college matches are usually played on unlighted courts after school and before dark; no-ad allows matches to be completed while there is enough daylight. Also, tournaments with large numbers of players, a restricted amount of time, and limited court space frequently use this method of scorekeeping.

The disadvantage of no-ad scoring is that the system penalizes the well-conditioned athlete. The player with good endurance can use longer games and sets to wear down an opponent. This does not happen as much in no-ad scoring. Because no game will last more than 7 points, it may be possible for a player who gets a good start to gain an edge that cannot be overcome in a short match.

Here is how the system works. The first player to win 4 points wins the game. Points are 1, 2, 3, and game, instead of 15, 30, 40, and game. There is no deuce or ad. When the score is tied at 3–3, the next point determines that game. At 3–3, the receiver chooses to receive the serve from either the right or left side.

Tie-Break Game

Tiebreakers were incorporated into the scoring system almost directly as a result of television. With traditional scoring, the length of matches is unpredictable. Sets have lasted for 30 and 40 games, and that drove the television people crazy. In order to sell advertising time and to manage programming schedules, *tie-break* games were introduced so that sets could come to a quick end when the set score reaches 6–6.

Tiebreakers work like this: In a 12-point tie-break game, the player or team that wins 7 points and is ahead by at least 2 points wins the game and that set. The score is called out as 1, 2, 3, 4, etc., throughout the game. A final tie-break score might be 7–0, 7–1, 7–2, 7–3, 7–4, 7–5, 8–6, 9–7, or so on.

The singles player (or the player on the doubles team) whose turn it is to serve, serves the first point from the right court. The opponent is the server for the second and third points, and after that, the players serve alternately for 2 consecutive points each until the

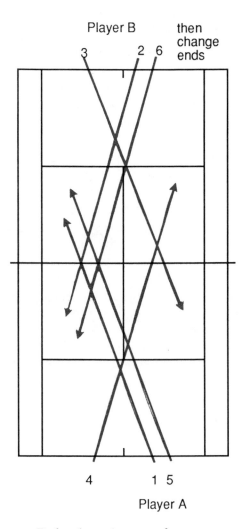

Figure 2 Tie-break serving procedures.

winner of the game and set has been decided. The second server serves the second and third points from the left and right courts, respectively, and this alternating continues until the tie-break game is completed. See Figure 2 for the rotation of servers and their positions.

Players change ends of the court after every 6 points and at the end of the tiebreaker. The player or team who served first in the tie-break game receives the serve in the first game of the next set.

Tennis Equipment

You do not have to invest a lot of money to start playing tennis. There are three kinds of equipment on the market. At one end of the market, there are cheap, poorly made products. At the other end, there are overpriced items whose quality does not match the cost. In the middle, you can find moderately priced, high-quality rackets, tennis balls, shoes, and clothes. Here are some suggestions to help you make the right decisions.

RACKETS

Tennis rackets range in price from $15 to $500. Starter rackets usually cost between $25 and $50. Serious players spend between $75 and $200 for their rackets. Once a certain price level is reached, the difference is one of personal preference, not of quality. A $300 racket is not necessarily better for you than one that costs $100. When you find the racket that is best for your budget and your style of play, stop looking. Sooner or later you have to hit the ball over the net, and the racket will be just about as good as you are.

The larger the hitting surface is, the better chance you have of making contact with the ball, and the larger the *sweet spot*—the area on the strings that gives the most smooth, powerful, controlled shot. However, some experts think that large hitting surfaces cause a *trampoline*, or rebound, effect on the ball, making it difficult to control.

Traditional-size rackets have a hitting surface of 60–79 square inches and represent less than 10% of recent sales. Midsize frames have from 80–95 square inches and have become increasingly popular. Oversize rackets have from 96–115 square inches and are used by players at all levels. Super-oversize rackets have more than 116 inches. Beginners should get a racket in the midsize or oversize range.

Wooden rackets are still on the market and can be purchased for reasonable prices, but they are not a good choice. They do not last as long as other rackets and do not offer the advantages of other products.

Metal rackets have been made of steel, titanium, magnesium, and aluminum. They are durable and easy to maneuver, but some of them vibrate on contact with the ball more than other frames. A racket that vibrates does not give the feel of hitting a solid shot, especially on shots that are hit off-center. In fact, the racket that vibrates on contact is probably not transferring your power to the ball as efficiently as it should.

Other products used to make rackets include fiberglass, graphite, boron, Kevlar, and ceramics. They are strong and light, and can be stiff or flexible. Most rackets are composites—made with two or more of the materials already mentioned. Products being combined allows you to select a racket that meets your needs in terms of balance, flexibility, stability, and feel. Most beginners buy aluminum or inexpensive composite rackets.

Rackets are classified as extra-light (XL), light (L), light-medium (LM), medium (M), and heavy (H). Table 1 shows the weight in ounces and grams of the racket classifications. Racket weights are usually quoted for unstrung frames, but many starter rackets are sold prestrung. Most beginners use rackets in the extra light or light categories.

Flexibility refers to how much the racket bends from end to end when you hit the ball. Some players can feel the frame *flex*, or give, when contact is made. Stiff frames give a little more control than flexible ones but may cause more elbow problems. Flexible rackets give more power and are easier on your arm, but it takes time to adjust to the feel of the frame.

Table 1 Racket Weights in Ounces and Grams

	ounces	grams	ounces	grams	
EXTRA LIGHT (XL)	11.0	311.8	12.6	357.1	LIGHT MEDIUM (LM)
	11.1	314.6	12.7	360.0	
	11.2	317.5	12.8	362.8	
	11.3	320.3	12.9	365.7	
	11.4	323.1	13.0	368.5	MEDIUM (M)
	11.5	326.0	13.1	371.3	
	11.6	328.8	13.2	374.2	
	11.7	331.6	13.3	377.0	
	11.8	334.5	13.4	379.8	
	11.9	337.3	13.5	382.7	
LIGHT (L)	12.0	340.1	13.6	385.5	HEAVY (H)
	12.1	343.0	13.7	388.3	
	12.2	345.8	13.8	391.2	
	12.3	348.6	13.9	394.0	
	12.4	351.5	14.0	396.8	
	12.5	354.3			

Ounces XL–under 12 oz. • L–12 to 12.5 oz. • LM–12.5 to 13 oz. •
M–13 to 13.5 oz. • H–13.51 oz. & over

Racket grips range in circumference from 4–5 inches. There are four ways to determine the right size for your hand:

- Shake hands with the racket or hold it with an Eastern forehand grip. As your fingers curl around the handle grip, the end of your thumb should touch the first joint of your middle finger (see Figure 3).

- Measure the distance from the long crease in your palm (second down from your fingers) to the tip of your ring finger. Position the ruler between your ring and middle fingers. The distance measured should be very close to the right grip size for your hand (Figure 4).
- Hold the racket in your playing hand. It should feel comfortable and easy to move.

Figure 3 The end of the thumb meets the first joint on the middle finger.

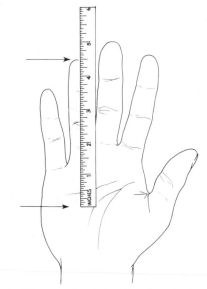

Figure 4 Measure from the tip of your ring finger to the second line in your palm.

The shape of the grip should fit the contour of your hand.

- Play with a demonstration or loaner racket. If it twists in your hand on contact, the grip may be too small. If your hand and arm tire quickly, it might be too big.

Most players use nylon or other synthetic strings. The 2% who use gut (beef intestine) are either very good players or are very serious about their games. Beginners should have rackets strung with nylon and can expect to pay $10 to $20 for a restringing job. Strings lose tension with or without play. If you play tennis twice a week, get your racket strung twice a year, even if a string does not break. If you play 5 times a week, have your racket strung about 5 times a year.

Most manufacturers recommend string tensions for their rackets. Larger racket heads should be strung at higher tensions—low 60s to the 80-pound range. Midsize rackets can be strung from the mid-50s to mid-60s, and standard-size frames are strung from the 40s to lower 60s.

Once you have selected the right racket and strings, take care of them. Rackets take a lot of abuse on the court during normal play. You can make them last longer and stay stronger by following these suggestions when you are not on the court:

- Do not store rackets in hot, cold, or damp places.
- Keep racket covers on rackets when they are not being used.
- Do not spin the racket on the court to determine serve and side; hold it in your hand to spin it, or let the other player spin.
- Do not place heavy objects on top of a racket.
- Do not use the racket to pick up balls, scraping the frame against the court.
- Wipe the strings clean after playing on a damp court or in high humidity.
- Clean grips with mild soap and water or with alcohol, then apply small amounts of mineral oil to keep the grip from drying.

- Do not throw your racket, bounce it off the court, or hit things (besides tennis balls) with it.
- Inspect your racket for warping or breaks before getting it restrung.
- If a string breaks, remove all the strings to relieve tension on the frame.

TENNIS BALLS

Tennis balls come in almost as many varieties as rackets. Do not start out with cheap ones and graduate to better quality balls as you improve. It is important to always play with good balls, so buy the best ones available the first time out. Brand names can be deceiving, but Penn, Wilson, Dunlop, Slazenger, and Spalding are some of the companies that make good tennis balls. Whatever the brand, look for information on the can that indicates the balls have been approved by the United States Tennis Association or the International Tennis Federation. Save money by watching for sales, shopping at discount stores, and buying a dozen or more balls at a time.

Most tennis balls are packaged in cans under pressure. When you open a can, you should hear a hissing sound, which is the pressurized air escaping. If you do not hear that sound, return the can to the dealer for a refund or a new can. If a ball breaks within the first 2 or 3 sets, the can of balls should be returned for replacement.

You can't play with one can of balls forever. Three balls may last two or three outings for beginners and some intermediates, but after that they begin to lose pressure and bounce, or the fuzz wears off. When that happens, use them for practice only. You can extend the life of balls by keeping them in the original container and by storing them in a cool place.

Some tennis balls are not packaged under pressure and are sold in a box. These balls are not as bouncy as those that are pressurized, but they never go completely dead. They eventually lose their fuzz, and this affects the bounce of the balls.

Ask for heavy-duty balls if you are going to play on hard surfaces like concrete. Regular "championship" balls are used on softer surfaces because they do not wear as quickly. You can also buy balls designed for play at high altitudes.

SHOES

The five factors to consider in buying tennis shoes are cost, durability, comfort, weight, and appearance. Shoes vary widely in price. Discount stores sell affordable shoes that will get you through a course or a series of lessons with no problems. If you plan to continue playing, it might be better to invest in a more expensive and more durable shoe.

How often you play, your style of play, and the court surface determine how much wear you get from your shoes. People who play often on hard surfaces may wear out a pair of shoes within a few weeks. Those who play on softer surfaces may get months out of their shoes. It is not unusual for the toe of one shoe to wear out completely while the rest of the shoe is still in good condition. Leather-topped shoes may be more comfortable than those with canvas, but they are also more expensive and may be heavier. If you are a player who wears out the sole or toe quickly, the comfort of leather may not be worth the expense.

Buy the lightest shoe possible if you are satisfied with the cost, comfort, and durability. A difference of a few ounces seems like pounds during the third set of a match.

For many people, the name and style of tennis shoes is more important than any other factor. If you are one of those people, remember that you may pay as much for the logo and the look as you do for durability and comfort.

CLOTHES

If you think tennis shoes reflect trends and advertising more than quality, wait until you shop for tennis apparel. The bad news is that you can spend a lot of money on shirts, shorts, skirts, warm-ups, and other active-wear clothing. The good news is that you can shop and find moderately priced, high-quality tennis outfits at sporting goods stores, department stores, discount stores, and some pro shops and specialty shops.

Students in physical education classes usually wear shorts and shirts approved by the school or college. Although there may be dress codes and conformity, there is no emphasis on fashion. If you take lessons or compete in other environments, there are guidelines to follow. Use your own common sense and ask a teacher, coach, tournament director, or pro what kind of dress is appropriate. The more time you spend at the tennis courts, the better feel you will have for dressing comfortably and to fit the occasion. Most serious players practice in the most comfortable clothes they can find. They play matches in the best looking outfits they can afford.

Warming Up for Success

The most traditional, and probably least effective, way to warm up is by hitting. It is the obvious way to get started, but there is a tendency not to exercise all of the muscles until actual play or difficult drills begin. When that happens, there is a greater chance of injuries. A good warm-up period should prepare your body for strenuous activity without tiring you in the process. Look at your warm-up as having three phases: general warm-up, stretching, and hitting. Then, follow your practice with a cool-down.

WARM-UP

In the first phase, move around, increase your blood circulation and gradually begin to prepare your body for the demands you are going to put on it. A general warm-up can be accomplished with light calisthenics or, as in the program described here, jogging the lines.

Jog the Lines

- Stand facing the net where the baseline intersects the singles sideline on the left side of the court.
- Holding the racket, jog forward along the sideline, and touch the net with the racket.
- Backpedal to the service line, while still facing the net.
- Shuffle-step (step to the side with one foot, then slide the other foot across to meet it) to the center service line.
- Jog forward and touch the net with your racket.
- Backpedal to the service line, while still facing the net.
- Shuffle-step to the other singles sideline.

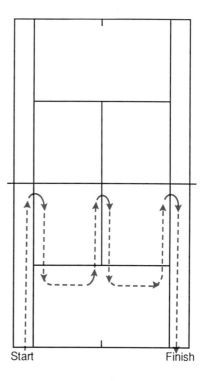

Start — Finish

- Jog forward and touch the net with your racket.
- Backpedal along the sideline to the baseline, while still facing the net.
- Walk slowly to the starting point and repeat the cycle.

STRETCHING

Stretch your muscles so they will be loose, warm, and ready to let you be as flexible as possible. Remember—DON'T STRETCH FIRST! The quickest way to injure a cold, tight muscle is to stretch it as far as it will go before it is ready. Loosen up first; stretch second.

Neck Stretch

Hold your neck and head upright. Stretch your neck by simply turning your head alternately to the right and left 10 times.

Upper Body Rotation

Clasp your hands together. Rotate your upper body to the right and left 10 times each, trying not to rotate your hips.

Achilles Tendon Stretch

Lean forward and down with both feet pointing straight, one foot ahead of the other, to stretch your Achilles tendon. Do not bounce, and keep your heels on the ground. Repeat 5 times, then lean forward on your other foot.

Groin Stretch

Lean forward and down, but point your front foot forward and your back foot to the side. Do not bounce. Repeat 5 times, then lean forward on your other foot.

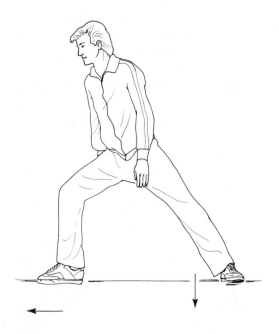

Lower Back and Hamstring Stretch #1

Stand with your knees slightly bent and feet together. Reach to grasp your legs as low as possible. Do not bounce. Hold for 5 seconds.

Lower Back and Hamstring Stretch #2

Sit on the floor with your legs extended. Reach forward and try to touch your ankles with your hands, and your chin to your knees. Hold for 5 seconds.

Inner Thigh Stretch

Sit with the soles of your feet touching. Try to touch your knees to the ground. Repeat 5 times.

Shoulder Girdle Stretch

Sit with your hands behind your body, knees flexed and feet flat on the court. Slide your hips forward without moving your hands. Repeat 5 times.

Service Stretch

Swing through the service motion 10 times with the racket cover still on your racket.

Shoulder Stretch

Hold your racket at the ends. Reach back behind your head as far as you can. Repeat 5 times.

HITTING

In the third warm-up phase, you should be ready to start hitting the shots you need to practice or play. Beginners should stay in the forecourt area and choose only the routines they can perform. Intermediate and advanced players can follow directions given and go through as many of the hitting combinations as time permits. Example hitting routines include:

- Start at midcourt. Softly keep the ball in play for 2 minutes (see Diagram 1).
- Move to the baseline. Hit controlled forehands and backhands for 2 minutes (see Diagram 2).
- Move to one side of the baseline. Hit down-the-line forehands for 2 minutes. Then, staying on that side, hit crosscourt forehands. Notice that forehand and backhand down-the-line hits and crosscourt hits occur on different sides of the court. Select the appropriate side dependent upon whether you are right- or left-handed (see Diagram 3).

- Move to the opposite side of the baseline. Hit down-the-line backhands. Then, staying on that side, hit crosscourt backhands (see Diagram 4).
- Move to the net. Hit forehand and backhand volleys down the middle of the court (see Diagram 5).
- Stay at the net. Hit controlled smashes while your partner moves to the baseline and hits controlled lobs. Then reverse positions. Practice starting from both sides of the net (see Diagram 6).
- Move to the baseline. Hit serves from the right and left sides (see Diagram 7).

COOL DOWN

After you have played or practiced, it is as important to get your body gradually back to normal as it is to move gradually into vigorous activity. Stopping all activity while the systems of your body are geared to operate at a higher level could cause problems with your circulatory system.

- After a match or practice session, walk the perimeter of the doubles court for 5 minutes or until your pulse rate drops below 120 beats per minute.
- Repeat any of the stretching exercises previously described.

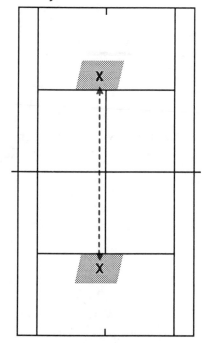

Diagram 1 Soft hits from midcourt positions.

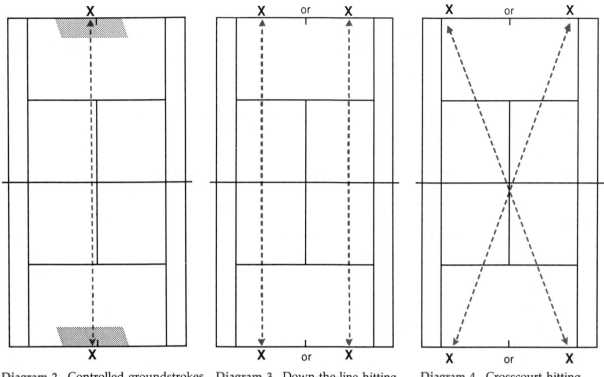

Diagram 2 Controlled groundstrokes from baseline positions.

Diagram 3 Down-the-line hitting positions.

Diagram 4 Crosscourt hitting positions.

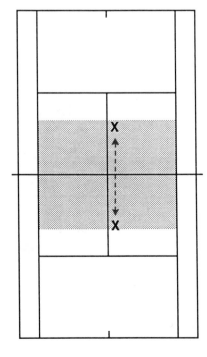

Diagram 5 Volley hitting positions.

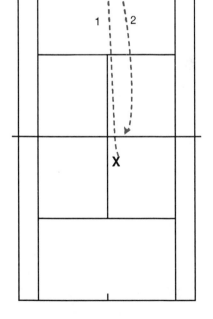

Diagram 6 Controlled smashes from a net position, then lobs.

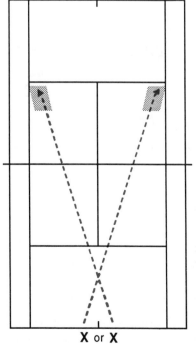

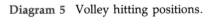

Diagram 7 Serving hitting positions.

Step 1 Handling the Racket

The first step in becoming a tennis player is getting used to the racket. The sooner it feels like an extension of your arm rather than an awkward piece of equipment, the sooner you can make it work for you. Before you start worrying about the strokes you use in tennis, get used to the way the racket feels and experiment with ways to use it.

The purpose in this step is not to learn about all the grips. Although the first drill will involve a forehand grip, details of the various ways to hold the racket for the forehand, backhand, serve, volley, and other shots will be discussed and illustrated later.

The activities that now follow should help you learn to use a tennis racket as you would any other tool. The order in which you do the drills in this step is not important (unlike in most steps). Racket-handling exercises can be done at the beginning of each class session or away from the courts at home or in a dorm room.

WHY IS HANDLING THE RACKET IMPORTANT?

Getting used to the racket establishes your feel for the distance between your hand and the face of the racket. While this may seem to be obvious, beginning players frequently miss the ball completely, hit it on the frame, or make contact somewhere other than on the middle of the strings. The exact kinds of exercises you now practice—hitting, stopping, bouncing, or even picking up tennis balls—do not really matter. The fact that you have the racket in your hand with something close to a proper grip and are using it instead of struggling with it shows that you are moving through the first step and will soon be ready for the second (see Figure 1.1). Improve your hand-eye coordination by making up your own racket-handling drills, or use the ones in this section.

Figure 1.1 Keys to Success: Handling the Racket

Execution Phase

1. Shake hands with racket
2. Keep ball at arm's length
3. Don't overswing or overhit

Racket-Handling Drills

1. Shake Hands Drill

Take turns with a partner, shaking hands with the racket handle to learn the Eastern forehand grip. Point one edge of the racket down toward the court. Shake hands with the racket. As you shake hands, your wrist is positioned slightly to the right of the top part of the grip for right-handers (slightly to the left for left-handers). Check your partner's grip and ask them to check yours.

Success Goal = 10 correct handshake grips with the racket

Your Score = (#) _____ "shake hands" grips

2. Tennis Ball Dribble Drill

Use an Eastern forehand grip and bounce the ball on the court, using the racket strings instead of your hand to dribble the ball. After you make contact with the ball, let your racket move up with the bounce of the ball before sending it to the court again.

Success Goal = 25 consecutive bounces

Your Score = (#) _____ bounces

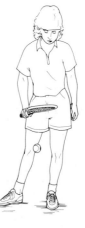

3. Air Dribble Drill

Use the Eastern forehand grip with your palm up. Bounce the ball a few inches into the air, using the strings to keep the ball going. Choke up on the racket if you cannot control the ball. Keep it low; you don't have to send it high into the air before the next bounce.

Success Goal = 25 consecutive "ups"

Your Score = (#) _____ "ups"

4. *Dribble the Lines Drill*

Using the Eastern forehand grip, dribble the ball around the court, trying to make the ball bounce on the lines bordering the singles backcourt. Slant your racket so that you direct the ball ahead of where you are now to a point where you will be after another step. If you dribble it straight down while walking forward, you will run over the ball and lose control.

Success Goal = 2 trips around the singles backcourt without losing control of the ball

Your Score = (#) _____ trips around the court

5. *String Catch Drill*

Have a partner softly toss a ball to the side of your body on which you hold your racket. Instead of hitting the ball, try to stop it with your racket strings, then catch it with your other hand before it hits the ground. Let the racket head give a little as you "catch" the ball. Make it a "soft" catch, not a hard one.

Success Goal = 7 out of 10 successful catches

Your Score = (#) _____ catches

6. Bump Tennis Drill

Stand about 20 feet from your partner and gently bump the ball back and forth to each other. Let it bounce in front of you as many times as necessary. Take a short backswing and let the racket do the work; hit the ball as gently as you can while bumping it toward your partner.

Variation: Place target tennis balls in front of you and your partner, then use the balls as targets as you bump to each other.

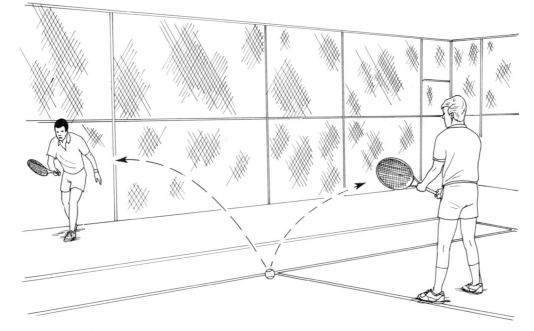

Success Goal = 2 minutes of bumps

Your Score = (#) _____ minutes

7. Net Bump Drill

Stand inside the service court and across the net from your partner. Bump the ball back and forth as many times as you can. Don't be intimidated by the net—the worst thing that can happen is that the ball will hit the net, and then you start over. Slant your racket up a bit to clear the net.

Success Goal = 4 bumps (after the bounce) in a row

Your Score = (#) _____ bumps

8. Ball Pickup Drill

Try to pick up a tennis ball off the court without using your free hand. Position the ball between the inside or outside of your foot and the head of your racket. Lift up quickly with both to get the ball off the ground. Get the edge of the racket under the ball, then move your racket up and bend your knee at the same time to lift the ball. Then dribble it once or twice with your racket strings to get it high enough to catch with your free hand.

Variation: Try to pick up a ball off the court by getting a dribble started with the racket strings making contact with the ball as it lies on the court. Hold your racket any way you want to, let the middle of the strings fall directly on top of the ball, raise your racket head slightly, and start the dribble. When the ball is high enough, catch it with your free hand. Don't worry about a forehand grip. Hold the racket like you would hold a frying pan until the ball is high enough to dribble with the "shake hands" grip.

Success Goal = 3 consecutive balls picked up

Your Score = (#) _____ pickups

9. Racket Edge Ups and Downs Drill

Practice bouncing the ball into the air using the racket edge pointing upward, or dribbling the ball on the court using the edge pointing down. Remember that you are doing this to become more comfortable with the racket and to see what it can do for you, not because you are going to hit shots with the edge of your racket.

Variation: Develop combinations of ups and downs, using both sides of the racket strings and both edges of the frame.

Success Goal =

    3 "ups" using the racket edge

    5 "downs" using the racket edge

Your Score =

    (#) _____ racket edge "ups"

    (#) _____ racket edge "downs"

Handling the Racket 19

Racket Handling
Keys to Success Checklist

Remember that the main purpose of this step is to begin to get used to the racket and to learn how to maneuver it. Don't worry if it feels a bit awkward at first; that is to be expected. Keep using the racket as an extension of your arm when you are on the court. Stop balls with the racket, use it to pick up balls off the court, point with it, dribble the ball with it between points, and invent other ways to use it. Practice on the courts before class begins, at home, or any other place where there is enough space. Now have your teacher or another trained observer watch and evaluate your racket-handling skills.

Execution
Phase

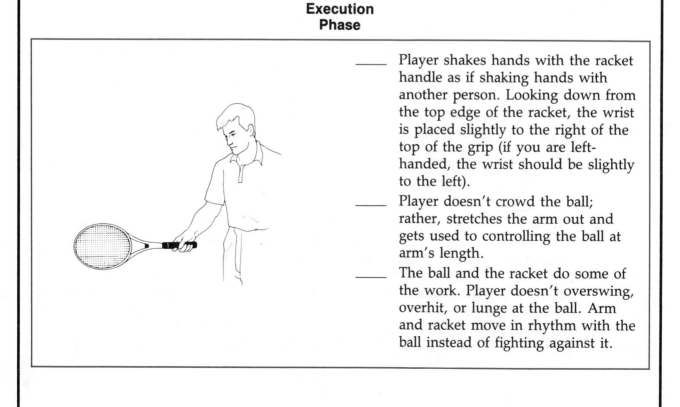

_____ Player shakes hands with the racket handle as if shaking hands with another person. Looking down from the top edge of the racket, the wrist is placed slightly to the right of the top of the grip (if you are left-handed, the wrist should be slightly to the left).

_____ Player doesn't crowd the ball; rather, stretches the arm out and gets used to controlling the ball at arm's length.

_____ The ball and the racket do some of the work. Player doesn't overswing, overhit, or lunge at the ball. Arm and racket move in rhythm with the ball instead of fighting against it.

Step 2   **Preparing to Hit**

One of the most common expressions heard from spectators when they are watching advanced players is "They really make it look easy." The reason good players make it look easy is that while most spectators are watching the ball being hit by one player, they do not see that the other player is working very hard to get into position for the next shot. By the time the average spectator looks, the hitter has prepared so well that there is nothing left to do but to swing at the ball.

Good tennis players prepare to hit also by blocking everything out of sight except the ball, the court, and the opponent. This is a difficult skill to learn, but even beginners can begin to master it.

WHY IS PREPARING TO HIT IMPORTANT?

Getting ready is as important as hitting. When you prepare well for each shot, you are in a good tactical position on the court, are in a comfortable position to hit the ball, and can choose from a variety of shot alternatives. The idea is to work hard between shots so you can relax and concentrate during the shot.

Though teachers will tell you things like "Be ready," "Watch the ball," and "Turn your side to the net," those expressions can be interpreted in many ways. Basically, as you learn what the most comfortable and productive body positions are for hitting all the different strokes, try to figure out ways to get to those positions early. You don't have to look like every other tennis player as you move and prepare to hit; one way or another, though, you do have to physically be prepared to hit an effective shot. Listen to what your instructor says; then let your body put that advice into action.

As with the drills in Step 1, the order in which you perform the drills in this step is not as important as just doing them. Activities such as the Hand Dribble Drill are appropriate for beginners. Others in this section—Grounder Drill, for example—are practiced by players from beginning to world-class skill levels.

HOW TO GET READY FOR SHOTS

The *ready position* is one of the terms most frequently heard when beginners listen to teachers. It means squaring your feet to the net, deciding on how to hold your racket, bending your knees, and leaning forward. When you're in the ready position, you should be watching the ball leave your opponent's racket and expecting the ball to come back over the net every time.

Most shots are hit on the run or after you've run to get into a ready position. The latter is preferable. Run first, set up second, and hit third. Ideally, try to hit every groundstroke (balls hit after the bounce) from about the same body position. One way to get there is to shuffle laterally, sliding your feet alternately in the direction you want to go. If you are really in a hurry, simply turn and run by crossing over as if you were going to pivot forward, then pushing off hard with the other foot. In either case, when you get to the ball, plant your back foot (the one away from the net), and step in the direction you want to hit with your other foot.

As your opponent gets ready to hit, watch the face of his or her racket. Then focus on the ball as you move into position. If you can see the kind of spin on the ball as it approaches your side, you are doing a good job of watching the ball. You are not able to see the ball hit your strings, but set that as a goal anyway and track it as close to the point of contact as possible (see Figure 2.1).

Figure 2.1 Keys to Success: Preparing to Hit

Ready Position

1. Forehand or backhand grip
2. Racket and weight forward
3. Opposite hand supporting racket
4. Knees slightly bent

Moving to Hit

1. Shuffle for close shots
2. Cross-step, run for farther shots
3. Plant back foot
4. Pivot forward

Watching
the Ball

1. Watch opponent's racket face
2. Focus on ball spin or print
3. Track ball until contact

Detecting Errors in Preparing to Hit

Problems with preparation are not usually evident until the shot has been attempted and missed. Detecting errors is difficult without a teacher or observer to help. Just keep in mind that the problems with any stroke might not be in the stroke itself, but in how you prepare (or do not prepare) to hit the ball.

ERROR	CORRECTION
1. You don't have enough time to hit.	1. Start in the ready position, then immediately return to that position after the hit. Start your backswing before the ball bounces on your side of the court.
2. You don't get to the ball in time.	2. After a shot, return to a central position or to an open part of the court. Do not leave daylight for your opponent to hit to.
3. You use an incorrect grip.	3. Use your opposite hand to help maneuver the racket and change grips when necessary.
4. Off-center hits occur.	4. Focus on the ball as long as possible. Try to read the print on the ball or to see the seams. Even though it is physically impossible, also try to see it hit the racket strings.

ERROR	CORRECTION
5. You make inconsistent shots.	5. Hustle to get into a comfortable position to hit. The more movement you make while hitting, the more things that can go wrong with your shot.
6. You hit into the net or not deeply enough into your opponent's court.	6. Try to move forward on all shots; retreating or hitting off your back foot causes a lack of power and a weak, shallow shot.

Preparation Drills

1. Grounder Drill

Stand 12 feet from your partner, who holds two tennis balls and alternately rolls them to your right and left sides. Move to the side, field one ball, roll it back, then move to the left to field the second ball.

As you move, do not cross your feet; learn to move with a shuffle step when you travel short distances. Keep your hips low to the ground by bending at the knees—not at the waist.

Success Goal = 45 seconds of play without making an error

Your Score = (#) _____ errors in 45 seconds

2. Side-To-Side Drill

Hold your racket and stand in the middle of the service court near the net. Move as fast as you can back and forth from the singles sideline to the center service line.

As you get ready to change directions, learn to plant one foot and use it to push off in the opposite direction. Be sure to cross the center service line with both feet. This is a skill you will use thousands of times as a tennis player.

Variation: Compete against a partner to see how many times you each cross the center service line in 30 seconds.

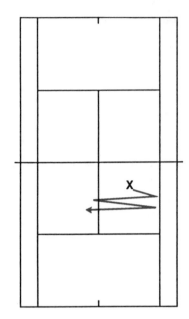

Success Goal = cross the line 10 times in 30 seconds

Your Score = (#) _____ times across the line

3. Wave Drill

Start at the center mark on the baseline. Have a partner stand 20 feet in front and signal you to move forward, backward, right, or left. Carry the racket in the ready position and move in the direction indicated. Use the shuffle step when moving to the side.

Keep your head up and stay under control. Make your body flow in any direction you want it to, rather than jerking around the court.

Success Goal = 45 seconds without stopping

Your Score = (#) _____ seconds without stopping

4. Shuffle Off to Buffalo Drill

Take a ready position, use the shuffle step to move to either side, then plant your back foot and pivot forward. Return to the starting place and to your ready position, then shuffle to the opposite side.

   Find a comfortable rhythm in your movement. You should reach a point where you can do this with your eyes closed, but don't try that in a match.

Success Goal = 10 repetitions to each side

Your Score = (#) _____ repetitions

5. Fly Drill

Have a partner throw or hit a variety of shots from the opposite court baseline or service line. Start at the center of your baseline without a racket and move to catch balls with your racket hand after one bounce. Move to where the ball will come down *after* the bounce—not to where it will first bounce.

Variation: Compete against a practice partner. The higher number of consecutive catches wins.

Success Goal = 10 consecutive catches

Your Score = (#) _____ catches

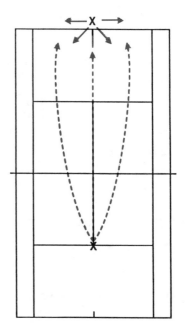

6. See the Seams Drill

Without a racket, toss the ball above your head, let it drop to the court, and try to read the print on the ball or see the seams as it moves. Catch it after one bounce; perform this drill 10 times.

If you think it will help, open your eyes wide to see the ball. Do anything you can to focus on the ball, while blocking out everything else.

Success Goal = read the print or see the seams 10 times

Your Score = (#) _____ times you see the print or seams

7. Hand Dribble Drill

Without a racket, bounce the ball with one hand 10 times, then 10 times with the opposite hand, and finally 20 times alternating hands with each dribble. Try to read the print on the ball or see the seams with each dribble. Let your hand move up and down with the ball to keep it going.

Success Goal = 40 total dribbles, reading the print or seeing the seams each time

   10 with one hand

   10 with opposite hand

   20 dribbles alternating hands

Your Score =

   (#) _____ dribbles with one hand

   (#) _____ dribbles with opposite hand

   (#) _____ dribbles alternating hands

8. Catch Drill

Without a racket, stand facing a partner 20 feet away. Take turns tossing the ball to each other using an underhand motion. Read the print or see the seams with each toss. Continue for 30 throws.

Take a step forward with your opposite foot when making the toss. Watch the ball all the way into your hands. Try to see it disappear as you catch it.

Variation 1: Use an overhand throwing motion.

Variation 2: Throw a soft bounce pass.

Success Goal = 30 tosses and catches without a miss

Your Score = (#) _____ tosses and catches

9. Toss Tag Drill

You and your partner take positions inside the same service court. One of you starts the drill by tossing a ball at least waist high that will bounce inside the service court if allowed to drop. The other player tries to get to the ball and catch it before it hits the court. That player immediately tosses it anywhere else in the service court, making sure that the ball is tossed at least waist high. Balls that bounce outside the court are not allowed.

The first player to make 10 catches (leading the opponent by at least 2 catches) wins. Move without stopping. Try to anticipate where your partner will toss the next ball. Don't watch anything but his or her hand and the ball. A common error is diagrammed on the right.

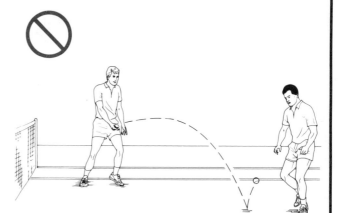

Success Goal = 10 consecutive catches

Your Score = (#) _____ catches

10. Double Toss Drill

Stand a few feet from your partner and gently toss two balls simultaneously to your partner. If he or she can catch both balls at the same time and return them so you can do the same thing, take one step back and repeat the exercise.

Remember—you are working as a team. Don't try to make it difficult. Toss softly and use your eyes to see both objects moving toward your hands.

Success Goal = 10 consecutive tosses and catches

Your Score = (#) _____ tosses and catches

Preparing to Hit
Keys to Success Checklist

Now that you have tested yourself by reaching the Step 2 Success Goals, ask your teacher, coach, pro, or another trained observer to evaluate your technique according to the checklist below. As you demonstrate the ready position, hold the racket directly in front of your body, use your opposite hand to support the racket at the throat, and lean forward. On almost every shot you hit, think about moving your feet first. Finally, learn to focus on the ball from the time your opponent hits it until the ball leaves your racket.

Ready Position

_____ The racket is held with an Eastern forehand or backhand grip.

_____ On the forehand, the V formed by the thumb and forefinger is slightly to the right of the top of the racket handle (for right-handers).

_____ Player slightly extends arms and racket forward.

_____ Player pushes forward with arms toward opponent.

_____ Player gets elbows away from ribs.

_____ Opposite hand supports the racket at the throat.

_____ Player readjusts grip following every shot. Having the other hand on the throat makes that adjustment easier.

_____ Player comfortably bends knees, doesn't stand with stiff legs. If the player thinks about leaning forward and expecting action, flexing the knees should not be a problem.

Moving to Hit

_____ Player uses a shuffle step for close shots, gliding to the ball without crossing feet.

_____ Player turns and runs for shots farther away, using a quick shoulder turn to get body in motion, then crossing over the front of body with a hard, fast first step.

_____ Player pivots forward in the direction of the target with the other foot. When getting to the ball, player plants the foot that is farther away from the net and steps toward the net with the other one, doesn't retreat or take a reverse pivot unless having no other choice. Player gets into the habit of transferring weight forward before making the shot.

Watching
the Ball

_____ Player watches opponent's racket face as he or she makes contact with the ball. Watching the other player's eyes or feet can fool the player. The ball has to come off of the strings, so the player must keep his or her eyes on that part of the racket.

_____ Player focuses on the ball as it approaches and tries to see the spin. It will either roll toward the player in the air like the tire on a car, spin on its side like a top, or spin in reverse.

_____ Player tries to see the ball make contact with strings. The human eye is not quick enough to actually see that happen, but the player can follow the ball as long as possible before contact.

Step 3 **Groundstrokes**

A *groundstroke* is a shot hit after the ball bounces on the court. A *forehand* groundstroke comes toward the side of your body where you hold your racket. It is the most frequently hit shot in tennis and the easiest to learn. The *backhand* groundstroke comes toward the side of the body opposite that on which you hold your racket. Although it is a natural stroke for some players, the backhand is generally considered to be harder to learn and a potential weakness for opponents to exploit.

WHY ARE GROUNDSTROKES IMPORTANT?

At least half of the shots hit in tennis are forehands. Because you will be hitting thousands of forehands, and because this shot can become a dangerous weapon in your tennis arsenal, its importance is obvious. Groundstrokes not hit with a forehand have to be hit with a backhand. If your backhand is weak, expect to see many more shots directed to that side of your body; if your backhand is adequate, opponents won't pick on it; and if it's strong, you can use it as another way to win points.

HOW TO EXECUTE THE FOREHAND

With one edge of the racket pointing toward the court, shake hands with the racket as if you were going to shake hands with another person. Curl your fingers around the grip near its base. As you hold the racket out to the right side (if right-handed), your palm should be slightly behind the racket handle, your wrist should be slightly to the right of the top of the handle, and the V formed by your thumb and index finger should be above, but slightly toward the back part of, the grip for an Eastern forehand grip. Left-handers, hold the racket so that your wrist is slightly to the left of the top of the grip as you look down over the top.

As soon as you know the ball is going to the forehand side, begin the *backswing*. The backswing is made by bringing the racket back either in a straight line parallel to the court or in a slight up-then-down loop, to a position where the racket is a bit lower than waist high and pointing to the fence or wall behind the baseline. If the racket head can be seen behind your body by a person standing in front of you, it is probably too far back. Waiting to make the backswing after the ball bounces does not allow you enough time to adjust to unexpected bounces, spin, or velocity. If the racket is already back there when you move into position, all you have to worry about is hitting.

As the ball comes to your forehand side, move into a position so that your opposite shoulder points to the ball and your feet form a line approximately parallel to the sideline. Use the foot away from the net to push off; transfer your weight forward as you begin to swing at the ball. As you hit, make sure that your weight moves forward. Some players take a small step forward with the foot closer to the net just before they hit the ball.

The forward weight transfer is one of the most important parts of any groundstroke. If it is not part of the stroke, power will be provided only by the arm instead of by the entire weight of the body. That causes weak shots and a very tired arm before the match or practice session is completed. One way to determine whether your weight is on the foot closer to the net is to notice the position of the shoulder closer to the net. If this shoulder is about even with the other shoulder or is in a downward posture, your weight is forward. If the shoulder is pointing up, your weight is still on the rear foot.

Your racket should move parallel to the court or in a slightly upward trajectory during the forward swing. This upward and forward action puts a little topspin on the ball, which helps make consistent strokes and cause high bounces on the other side of the net. Make contact with the ball just before it reaches a point even with the midsection of your body. You won't be able to do this on every shot, but set it as a goal.

Keep your wrist firm and in a position that forms a curve with the top of your forearm. Do not let your wrist move during the swing. Think of sweeping something off of a table or ironing board. Extend your arm comfortably, but not completely, with the swing. Try to "carry" the ball on the racket strings. Hold the racket tightly enough so it does not twist on impact, but not so tightly that your feeling for the racket is lost.

After the hit, follow the ball with the racket. In this follow-through, try to reach out toward the net. When the racket cannot go any far-

ther forward, it should cross the front of your body and finish high, pointing in the direction of the shot.

Every time you hit a forehand, the total action in the swing should be about the same (see Figure 3.1). If the ball comes lower than your waist, bend your knees, keeping your back straight, and use the same motion. Do not stand straight up and "golf" at the ball. If the ball bounces deeply in the backcourt and high to your forehand, retreat quickly, plant your back foot, and move your weight forward with the swing. If a ball falls short in your court, move up, plant, step, swing, and follow through.

Figure 3.1   Keys to Success: Forehand

Preparation Phase

1. Eastern forehand grip
2. Draw racket back early
3. Turn side to net
4. Step toward target

**Execution
Phase**

e

f

1. Shift weight forward
2. Swing parallel to court
3. No wrist movement

4. Focus on the ball
5. Make contact early

**Follow-Through
Phase**

1. Continue swing after hit
2. Swing out, across, up
3. Point racket toward target

g

Detecting Errors in the Forehand

It is not enough to recognize that you are having problems executing a stroke such as the forehand. You or your instructor must also be able to make corrections to solve stroke problems. Here are some common forehand flaws and corrective suggestions.

ERROR 🚫

CORRECTION

ERROR	CORRECTION
1. There's not enough time to hit.	1. Start preparing when the ball leaves your opponent's racket; don't wait until it bounces on your side.
2. You hit shots too hard or too deep.	2. Reduce the length of your backswing. Keep the racket face perpendicular to the court.
3. Your forehand lacks power.	3. Your weight should be forward when you make contact. Take a level backswing and swing forward through the ball; no follow-through causes a short, weak shot.
4. There is general inconsistency.	4. Check your grip and keep your wrist in a fixed position; the more movement, the less control.

HOW TO EXECUTE THE BACKHAND

There are at least three acceptable ways to hold the racket for a backhand. The most common grip is the *Eastern backhand*. With this grip, a right-hander's wrist should be slightly to the left of the top of the racket handle (looking down on the racket, with its edges perpendicular to the court); a left-hander's wrist is slightly to the right of the top. Think of your thumb as having a top, bottom, outside, and inside. The inside part of the thumb should be in contact with the back, flat part of the racket handle. There are several ways in which you might align your thumb along that part of the grip, but it is essential that the inside part be in contact with the racket. During a point, the thumb's position may change, but the part touching the grip should not (see Figures 3.2a and b).

Figure 3.2a Right-handed Eastern backhand grip.

Figure 3.3a Right-handed Continental grip.

Figure 3.2b Left-handed Eastern backhand grip.

Figure 3.3b Left-handed Continental grip.

Players with strong forearms may want to use the *Continental* grip. Here the wrist is directly on top of the racket handle (looking down over the top). Your thumb has to provide more support from the rear because your wrist is not positioned behind the racket. Extend your thumb along the back of the grip so that the inside part is in contact, pushing against the racket handle during the stroke. The advantage of holding the racket this way is not having to change grips from the forehand to the backhand. The disadvantage is that some players feel uncomfortable hitting shots on either side of the body because the Continental grip is halfway between the conventional forehand and backhand grips (see Figures 3.3a and b).

The *two-handed backhand* is effective for many players. It gives added power, a controlled swing, and a better racket position to hit with topspin. The disadvantages are not being able to reach as far for wide shots, not being able to maneuver the racket easily on shots hit directly at you, and not developing strength in the dominant arm.

There are two ways to hold the racket for the two-handed stroke. The simplest is to hold an Eastern forehand with one hand and to add a forehand grip with the other. The two hands are then touching each other, as the fingers are spread along the racket grip. Some players prefer to hold a regular backhand grip with the strong hand, then add a forehand grip with the other. Either method is okay; just find the style most comfortable for you (see Figures 3.4a and b).

Regardless of how you hold your racket, start taking it back as soon as the ball leaves

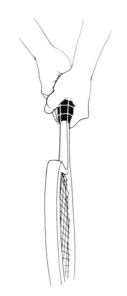

Figure 3.4a Right-handed two-hand backhand grip.

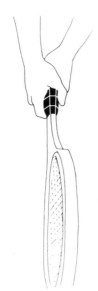

Figure 3.4b Left-handed two-hand backhand grip.

the other player's racket. Use your nonracket hand to cradle the racket at its throat or shaft. Leave that hand on the racket throat during the entire backswing unless you are using a two-handed stroke. As the racket goes back, rotate your shoulders far enough so that your opponent can see your back. Bring your racket back in a line parallel to the court or slightly below your waist. Think of drawing a sword out of your pocket. Learn to prepare to hit as you move. Do not wait until the last second.

Turn before contact so that your opposite shoulder is pointing in the direction of the target. Bend your knees slightly. The foot closer to the net may be pointing toward the sideline, or it may be at a 45-degree angle to the net. For added power, take a small step forward with the foot closer to the net just before you make contact. Lean forward with the swing. Remember that if the shoulder closer to the net is up, the weight is still on the rear foot. If it is down, though, the weight can be transferred forward.

Swing in a line approximately parallel to the court. If you want topspin, start the racket head lower and swing upward; put backspin on the ball by starting with the racket a bit higher than the waist. In any case, keep your wrist firmly in place throughout the swing. The racket head should be higher than your wrist on all but very low shots. Make contact with the ball even with, or in front of, the foot closer to the net. This gives more power and allows you to use the pace put on the ball by the other player. Two-handers can wait longer to make contact.

Follow through out toward the net, across the front of your body, and up—in that order. Think of reaching out for the net with the back of your hand, then bring the racket across. Finish the stroke by pointing in the direction of the target (see Figure 3.5).

Figure 3.5 Keys to Success: Backhand

Preparation Phase

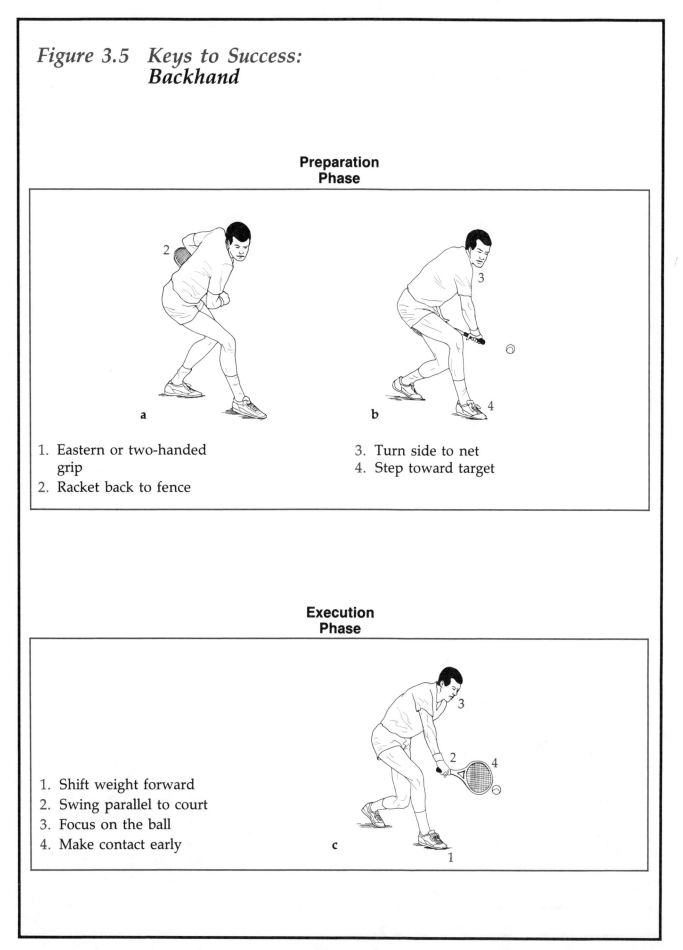

1. Eastern or two-handed grip
2. Racket back to fence

3. Turn side to net
4. Step toward target

Execution Phase

1. Shift weight forward
2. Swing parallel to court
3. Focus on the ball
4. Make contact early

**Follow-Through
Phase**

1. Continue swing after hit
2. Swing out, across, up

3. Point toward target

Detecting Errors in the Backhand

Backhand errors fall into the same general categories as those with the forehand. They usually involve poor preparation, the wrong grip, leading with the elbow, or not following through.

ERROR 🚫

CORRECTION

1. You don't have enough time to hit.

2. You hit shots too high.

1. Get to the ball early. Set up by lining up your feet parallel to the sideline. Lean into the shot.

2. Check the angle of your racket; the face should be perpendicular to the court.

ERROR	CORRECTION
3. Backhand lacks power.	3. Don't try to hit a backhand with a forehand grip. Follow through. Develop strength by taking more shots on that side.
4. You lead with your elbow.	4. Keep your elbow closer to your waist. Let the racket head lead the stroke.
5. You hit shots to the side.	5. Make contact earlier; don't let the ball get even with your body.
6. There is general inconsistency.	6. Reduce the length of your backswing; the less movement, the less chance of error.

Groundstroke Drills

1. Mirror Drill

Practice alternating the forehand and backhand swings in front of a mirror. Say to yourself, "Ready, pivot, step, swing." Develop a smooth motion as you pretend to hit.

Success Goal = 50 alternating forehand and backhand swings using the Keys to Success fundamentals

Your Score = (#) _____ alternating swings

2. Drop and Hit Forehand Drill

Stand with your nonracket shoulder toward the net. Drop a ball (don't throw it down) to your forehand side, let it bounce, then hit it over the net with a forehand stroke.

   Few players put the ball in play by dropping and hitting with a backhand; it is more comfortable and practical with a forehand. Hit the ball a safe distance over the top of the net and try to hit it as far into the opposite backcourt as possible.

Variation 1: Drop the ball and let it bounce twice before you hit it.

Variation 2: Drop and hit to the backcourt target area.

Success Goal = 10 forehand groundstrokes into the target area

Your Score = (#) _____ forehand groundstrokes

3. Toss to Groundstroke Drill

Have a partner stand across the net without a racket at a distance of 20 feet. Your partner tosses balls first to your forehand and then to your backhand. Direct soft groundstrokes to your partner. Your partner should catch or reach your shot with at least one hand.

   Don't overswing. Work on control before worrying about power. Develop control early as a tennis player. If you are good enough to hit the ball at a tosser or hitter, you will be good enough to hit away from your opponent during a match.

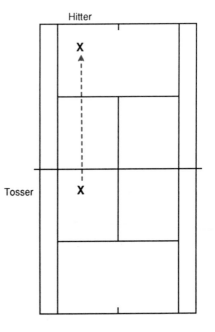

Success Goal = 15 consecutive groundstrokes caught by partner

Your Score = (#) _____ groundstrokes

4. Wall Ball Groundstroke Drill

Stand 20 feet from a wall. Try to keep the ball in play against the wall with softly hit forehands or backhands. Drop and hit to put the ball into play; don't let it stop. Again, the emphasis is on maintaining control of the ball, not trying to see how hard you can hit.

Success Goal =

15 consecutive forehands off wall

20 consecutive backhands off wall

Your Score =

(#) _____ forehands

(#) _____ backhands

5. Alternating Wall Ball Groundstroke Drill

Repeat Drill 4, but alternate hits against the wall with a practice partner. Hit, then use a shuffle step to get out of the way for your partner to hit. Do not turn your back to the wall. Remember: Hit and move!

Success Goal =

20 consecutive forehands

20 consecutive backhands

Your Score =

(#) _____ forehands

(#) _____ backhands

6. Forehand Service Court Rally Drill

Stand on or behind the service line; turn your side to the net, then drop and softly hit a forehand to a partner on the other side. Keep the ball in play, hitting all shots so that they bounce into the opposite service court.

As soon as you hit one shot, start preparing for the next one by using your opposite hand to adjust your grip and by moving your feet to return to a central position behind the service line. Resist the temptation to move inside the service line after every shot. If you do, shots will come at your feet too often. It is easier to move forward to get to short shots than to move backward to return deep ones.

Success Goal = 20 consecutive hits between partners

Your Score = (#) _____ hits

7. Backhand Service Court Rally Drill

Repeat Drill 6, but keep the ball in play with backhand groundstrokes. Even though you expect to hit backhands, get back to a ready position with your hands and your feet. In competition, you won't have the luxury of knowing where the ball will be hit.

Success Goal = 20 consecutive hits between partners

Your Score = (#) _____ hits

8. Service Court Groundstroke Game

Repeat either Drill 6 or Drill 7, keeping score with the no-ad system. Drop the ball to put it into play. The first player to win 4 points wins the game.

Now you can hit away from the other player. Don't hit hard; just try to place the ball to open areas of the court.

Success Goal =

play 2 out of 3 games, 3 out of 5 games, or complete a set

Your Score =

(#) _____ games won

(#) _____ games lost

9. Baseline Setup Drill

Take a position at the baseline and have a partner put balls into play to either your forehand or your backhand. Return the ball to the opposite backcourt.

Work on depth as well as technique. The key to getting the ball deep is to hit it higher over the net, not just to hit it with more power.

Success Goal =

10 forehands

10 backhands hit to the backcourt

Your Score =

(#) _____ forehands

(#) _____ backhands

10. Baseline Rally Drill

Stand on or behind the baseline. Drop the ball to put it into play, and keep it in play by hitting into the opposite singles court. Concentrate on the ball—not your opponent, the net, or any other distraction (there will be plenty of time for that later).

Success Goal = 20 consecutive hits between you and your partner

Your Score = (#) _____ hits

11. *Runaround Groundstroke Drill*

Stand several steps to the forehand side of the center mark at the baseline, facing the net. Have a partner hit 3 consecutive shots—the first one to your forehand in the corner where you begin the drill, the second down the middle of the court, and the third to the opposite corner. Get to and hit all 3 shots with a forehand groundstroke. Run around your backhand to do it. Then, from the corner where you finish the series of 3 shots, return 3 more (corner, middle, opposite corner) with backhands.

Tennis is frequently a game of emergency situations. You will not always have the luxury of being in exactly the right position to hit groundstrokes. Use this drill to practice hitting in difficult positions and to improve your footwork.

Success Goal = 6 consecutive shots returned

Your Score = (#) _____ shots

12. *Crank It Up Drill*

Start at the baseline and have a partner feed shots into your backcourt area. Return the first 10 shots at 50% velocity on both the forehand and backhand sides. Return the next 10 at 75%. Then return the last 10 shots hitting as hard as you can while retaining accuracy.

One indication of your growth as a player is your ability to hit the ball at different speeds. This drill helps you develop that ability.

Success Goal =

   10 forehand and backhand returns at 50% speed off of 10 feeds

   6 returns at 75% speed off of 10 feeds

   3 returns at 100% speed off of 10 feeds

Your Score =

   (#) _____ returns at 50% speed

   (#) _____ returns at 75% speed

   (#) _____ returns at 100% speed

13. *Topspin Drop and Hit Drill*

Stand at the baseline. Turn your nonracket side to the net and draw your racket back so that it almost touches the ground behind you. Drop a ball to the forehand side and swing forward and up, keeping the racket face perpendicular to the court. Hit forehands into the opposite court with topspin. Watch the ball to see that rotation is made after contact. Call out the type of spin you see—topspin, backspin, or sidespin.

   If you can choose when to hit with topspin, you have moved out of the beginner stage and into a higher level of skill.

Success Goal = 5 out of 10 attempts hit with topspin

Your Score = (#) _____ hits with topspin

14. *Topspin Rally Drill*

Stand at the baseline and keep the ball in play for 1 minute with a partner, hitting topspin forehands. Watch the ball after contact to see the rotation. Call out the type of spin you see.

   You will not be able to use topspin on every shot; use good judgment in choosing the right time to try it.

Success Goal = 10 topspin forehands in 1 minute

Your Score = (#) _____ topspin forehands

Forehand
Keys to Success Checklist

Before someone evaluates your forehand technique, try to imagine how you should look as you prepare, swing, and follow through. Get the racket back early and with a smooth motion, sweep at the ball as if you were sweeping dishes off a table (movement at the shoulder—not at the elbow or wrist), and hold your follow-through as if posing for a picture. Concentrate on technique now; accuracy and power will come later. Now have a trained tennis observer check your forehand form.

Preparation
Phase

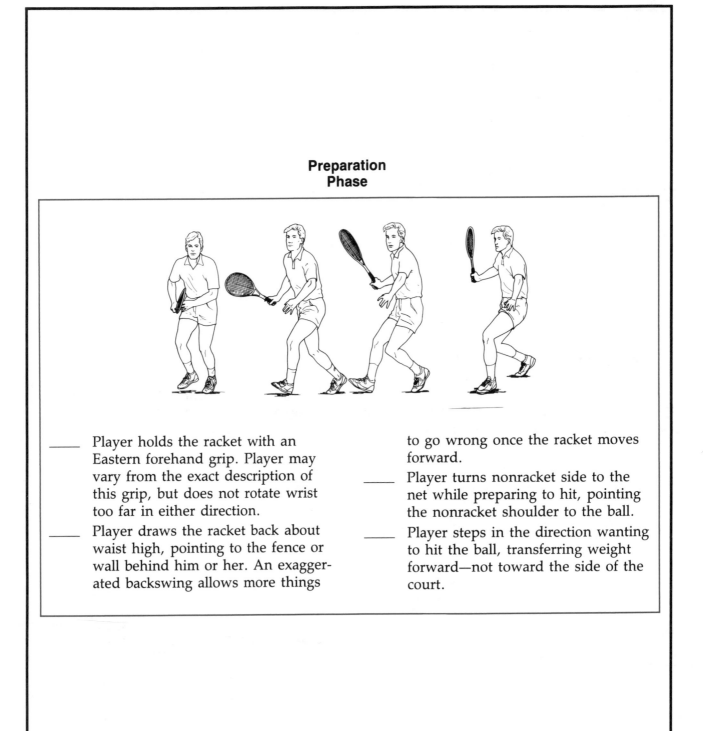

_____ Player holds the racket with an Eastern forehand grip. Player may vary from the exact description of this grip, but does not rotate wrist too far in either direction.

_____ Player draws the racket back about waist high, pointing to the fence or wall behind him or her. An exaggerated backswing allows more things to go wrong once the racket moves forward.

_____ Player turns nonracket side to the net while preparing to hit, pointing the nonracket shoulder to the ball.

_____ Player steps in the direction wanting to hit the ball, transferring weight forward—not toward the side of the court.

Execution
Phase

_____ Player leans forward and shifts weight forward while swinging. Player should think of leaning into a wave at the beach.

_____ Player swings racket forward in a motion approximately parallel to the court—like a door opening, then closing.

_____ Wrist stays firm during swing. The back of the forearm and the top of the hand form a slight curve—not a straight line.

_____ Player focuses on the ball and tries to watch it all the way into racket strings.

_____ Head stays down and still until after the ball leaves racket.

_____ Racket makes contact with the ball early, before it gets even with the body.

Follow-Through
Phase

_____ Player continues swinging after hitting the ball. A fluid swing continues after the shot; it doesn't stop with the hit.

_____ Player swings out toward the net, across the front of the body, and upward—in that order.

_____ Swing finishes by pointing in the direction of hit. Player poses for a picture for a split-second after the swing.

Backhand
Keys to Success Checklist

Keep the nonracket hand on the throat of the racket between shots. While it may not seem important now, as you begin to change grips from forehand to backhand, the other hand will be there to help you maneuver the racket. Get ready early by moving your feet into a comfortable, balanced position, and by drawing your racket back to point at the fence or wall behind the court. Reach out toward the net as you swing forward—don't cross the front of your body with the racket too soon. Hold the follow-through after the shot just as you did on the forehand. Ask your teacher, coach, or pro to evaluate your backhand technique.

Preparation Phase

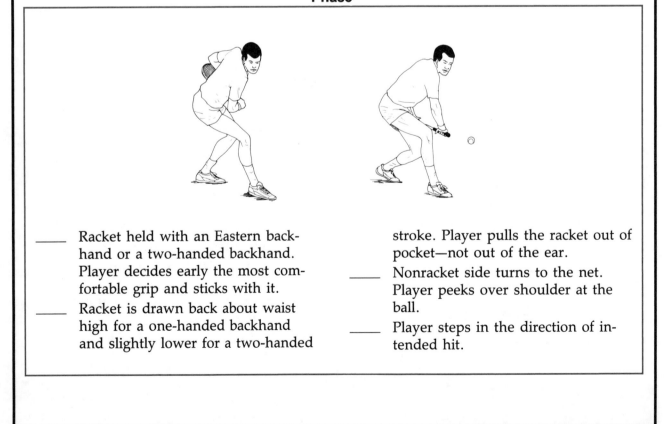

_____ Racket held with an Eastern backhand or a two-handed backhand. Player decides early the most comfortable grip and sticks with it.

_____ Racket is drawn back about waist high for a one-handed backhand and slightly lower for a two-handed stroke. Player pulls the racket out of pocket—not out of the ear.

_____ Nonracket side turns to the net. Player peeks over shoulder at the ball.

_____ Player steps in the direction of intended hit.

Execution
Phase

_____ Player leans and shifts weight forward before or during swing. Either way, weight is on the front foot—not the back.

_____ Racket swings forward in a motion that is approximately parallel to the court or slightly upward.

_____ Focuses on the ball, tries to follow it with eyes all the way into racket strings.

_____ Racket makes contact with the ball before ball gets even with body. Player lets racket go to the ball—doesn't let ball come to racket. Two-handers can wait a fraction of a second longer.

Follow-Through
Phase

_____ Player continues swinging after hitting the ball, swinging through the shot instead of stopping at the moment of contact.

_____ Swing goes out toward the net, across the front of body, and up-

ward. Player tries to touch the net with the back of hand.

_____ Swing finishes by pointing in the direction of hit. Player counts to 2 on the follow-through.

Step 4 Groundstroke Combinations

Once the ball has been put into play, you repeatedly hits shots from a variety of locations along the baseline. Here are some suggestions to help you develop your baseline game:

- Change grips between forehand and backhand strokes.
- Use your nonracket hand to adjust grips between shots.
- Return to a central position (usually the center mark on the baseline) between shots.
- Work hard to get into proper position between shots.
- Be patient and keep the ball in play. You win more points when your opponent makes an error than when you hit winners.

WHY ARE GROUNDSTROKE COMBINATIONS IMPORTANT?

Whether you are hitting with a friend, going through drills in a practice session, warming up, or actually playing a match, the one thing that tennis players do most is hit balls back and forth from the baseline. Although serves, volleys, lobs, smashes, and other shots are important parts of the game, nothing is more important or more basic to tennis than being able to keep the ball in play from the baseline. Now that you have progressed through the forehand and backhand steps separately, your next step is to hit both groundstrokes consistently enough to play points.

Groundstroke Combination Drills

1. Running Groundstroke Drill

Have a partner stand at the net with a basket of balls and toss or hit balls alternately to your forehand, then backhand. Count the number of consecutive shots you return into the singles court. Use your opposite hand to maneuver the racket, and change grips between strokes.

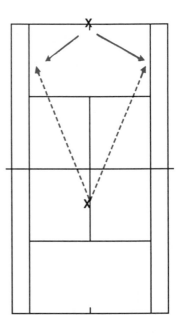

Success Goal = 20 consecutive groundstrokes into the target area

Your Score = (#) _____ groundstrokes

2. Groundstroke Games

Drop a ball and put it into play against a partner. Keep it in play for at least 2 shots before trying to win the point. Every shot has to be hit with a groundstroke. First player to win 10 points wins the game.

Look for openings on the other side of the court. Once the ball has been hit twice, hit to where your opponent *is not*, rather than where he or she *is* on the court.

Variation: Increase the minimum number of ''in'' shots before trying to win a point.

Success Goal = win at least half the games played

Your Score = (#) _____ games won

3. Footwork Drill

Start in the middle of your service line and have a partner sit down across the net with a basket of balls. Your partner tosses shots anywhere inside the service court for 1 minute. Every time you hit, another ball is immediately tossed to another spot in the court.

Use short steps, short bursts of speed, and short strokes to get the ball back. Worry more about footwork than strokes.

Success Goal = return every shot attempted for a 1-minute period; missing zero is perfect.

Your Score = (#) _____ shots missed

4. Two-Minute Drill

Start at the baseline. Return balls tossed or hit by your practice partner to your forehand and backhand for a 2-minute period.

Force yourself to get to every shot, no matter how far away it is. Don't worry about how you look; worry about covering the court and doing whatever it takes to get the ball back.

Success Goal = return at least half the shots attempted during a 2-minute period

Your Score = (#) _____ returned shots out of (#) _____ attempted

5. Crosscourt Groundstroke Drill

Line up slightly to one side of the center mark. Keep the ball in play with your partner, hitting crosscourt shots only. Change your positions so that you practice both forehand and backhand shots.

Leave a space for your practice partner to hit. Don't start so far to either side that you are standing in the corner.

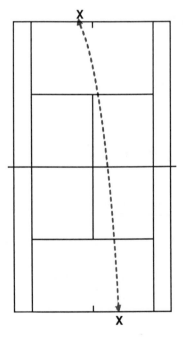

Success Goal = 100 total attempts between you and your partner (50 shots per player)

Your Score = (#) _____ attempts

6. Down-The-Line Groundstroke Drill

Keep the ball in play from the baseline area, hitting only down-the-line groundstrokes to your partner. Change positions so that you practice both forehand and backhand ground-strokes.

Don't aim at the sidelines. Leave room for error so that off-target shots still have a chance to go in.

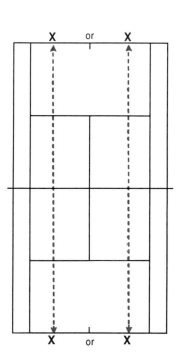

Success Goal = 100 total attempts between you and your partner (50 shots per player)

Your Score = (#) _____ attempts

7. Corner-to-Corner Drill

Start at the baseline center mark and have a partner set up a short shot to your forehand, followed by a deep shot to your backhand. Repeat the 2-shot series 5 times. Then change the sequence to hit a short backhand, then a deep forehand.

As soon as you hit one shot, change grips and start moving and preparing for the next one. Hit the first shot down the line closer to you; get the next back any way and anywhere you can—probably down the opposite line.

Variation: Have your partner hit the first shot very short, followed by a lob to the opposite corner. Let the lob bounce before returning it with a groundstroke or lob.

Success Goal = 5 sets of 2 forehands and backhands without an error

Your Score = (#) _____ sets of 2 groundstrokes without an error

Step 5 Beginner's (Punch) Serve

The *beginner's serve* is also called a *punch serve* or a *half-swing serve*. The beginning server uses it to put the ball into play to start a point. This type of serve enables you to start playing games and matches. It is not a power shot; as you get stronger and better as a tennis player, you will replace the punch serve with a full swing serve.

WHY IS THE BEGINNER'S SERVE IMPORTANT?

Any serve is important because a point cannot begin without one. Players alternate serving entire games throughout the match, so hitting yours into the proper service courts is not just important—it's vital. The sooner you can master the punch serve, the sooner you can move on to a more sophisticated and effective service motion.

HOW TO EXECUTE THE BEGINNER'S SERVE

Hold the racket with an Eastern forehand grip. It is comfortable and allows a reasonable amount of control over the ball. As your serving motion becomes more fluid, you can change your grip to accommodate the swing.

Stand at about a 45-degree angle to the net, so that you are facing one of the net posts. If you are right-handed, your left foot is forward and positioned at the angle just mentioned; if left-handed, your right foot is forward, closer to the net. The foot away from the baseline should be placed so that if a line were drawn from the toes of that foot to the toes of the foot closer to the baseline, the line would point in the direction you want to serve. Put your weight on the foot away from the baseline and spread your feet wider than the width of your shoulders.

Toss the ball slightly higher than you can reach with your racket. To measure the right height of your toss, extend your arm and racket upward as high as you can comfortably reach. Now put the racket a little in front, so that if something were to fall off of the racket, it would fall about 1 foot inside the baseline. With your arm and racket fully extended, you should toss the ball so it reaches a peak higher than the tip end of the racket. The toss has to be at that spot consistently. If any toss is not where you want it to be, catch the ball or let it drop to the court and start again. You can learn to toss the ball exactly to the right spot every time. When you do, this is one thing you do not have to worry about going wrong in your serving motion.

Tossing or lifting the ball for the serve also involves technique, as well as placement. Hold the ball at the base of the fingers in your tossing hand. Extend your arm in the direction you want to hit. Now lift your arm without bending it very much at the elbow. As you lift, release the ball at about head height by extending (opening) your fingers. The ball should go up without much spin. If it comes off of your fingertips or if you flip your wrist with the toss, the ball will have spin, and that causes a loss of control.

Hold your racket with the forehand grip, stand at an angle to the baseline, and now "scratch your back" with the racket by touching the middle of your back with the edge of your racket. Lift the racket head a few inches and from this starting point, swing up at the ball you have learned to toss. It is important that the serving motion goes up at first rather than forward. Do not let your elbow lead the stroke; keep it high until after the hit. When you hit, reach as high as you can. Your arm and racket should be fully extended when contact is made.

As you hit, your racket moves up and forward. After contact, the racket continues forward (toward the net) as far as it can go. The rest of the follow-through should be across the front of your body, ending low on the opposite side from which the motion began (see Figure 5.1).

Figure 5.1 Keys to Success: *Beginner's Serve*

Preparation Phase

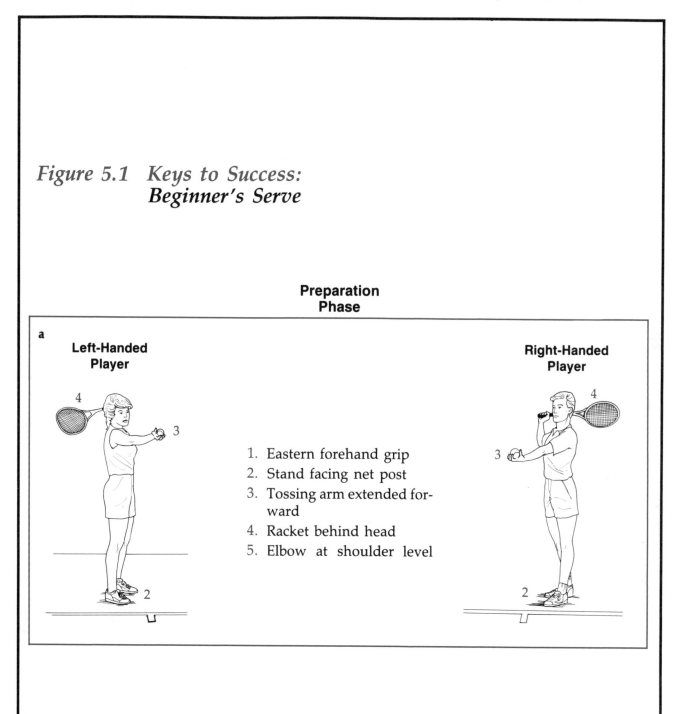

Left-Handed Player

Right-Handed Player

1. Eastern forehand grip
2. Stand facing net post
3. Tossing arm extended forward
4. Racket behind head
5. Elbow at shoulder level

Execution Phase

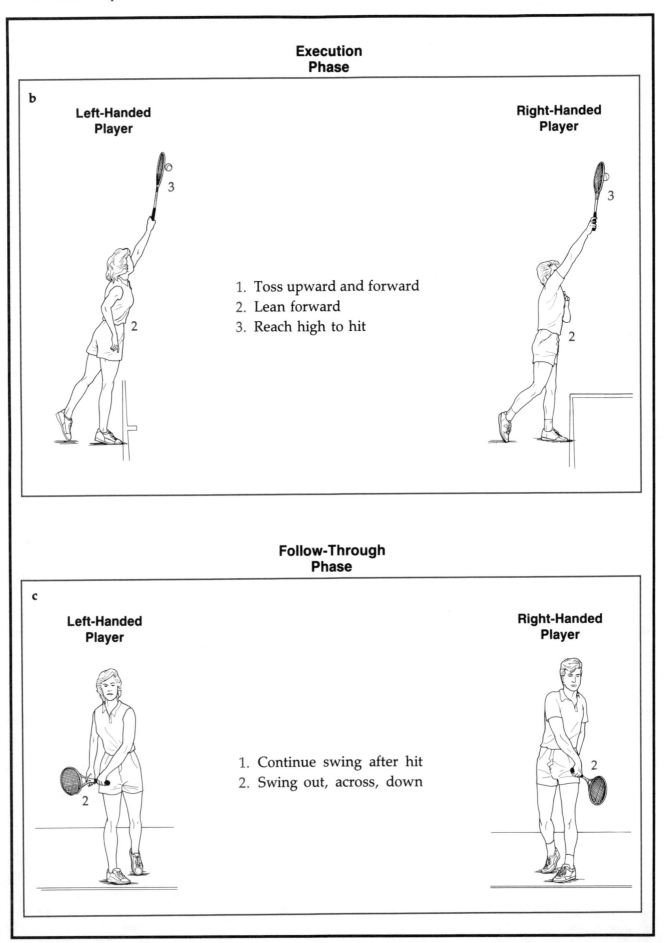

b

Left-Handed Player

Right-Handed Player

1. Toss upward and forward
2. Lean forward
3. Reach high to hit

Follow-Through Phase

c

Left-Handed Player

Right-Handed Player

1. Continue swing after hit
2. Swing out, across, down

Detecting Errors in the Beginner's Serve

Because this serve is simple and only a first step in the direction of a more advanced serve, do not expect too much from it. Problems are easy for you to recognize and relatively easy to solve. The real problems will begin when you move from the security of this serve to a more complicated, but more effective, intermediate serving motion.

ERROR ⊘

CORRECTION

ERROR	CORRECTION
1. Your serve lacks power.	1. Don't expect any. This motion provides accuracy—not power.
2. You serve into the net.	2. Toss the ball slightly higher than you can reach, then reach high to hit it; if you let the ball drop, the racket face will turn down and force the ball into the net.
3. You serve wide to the right or left.	3. Hold your racket with a forehand grip. The strings should direct the ball into the target area. Stand at a 45-degree angle to the baseline; a line drawn from the toes of one foot to the other should point in the direction of the service court.
4. There is general inconsistency.	4. Get a mental picture of how your racket should be positioned at the time of contact. Learn how to position your wrist, so that you become very consistent in hitting. Be deliberate in your approach to the serve; don't just walk up and take a hopeful swing at the ball.

Beginner's Serve Drills

1. Punch Serve Throw

Throw a tennis ball from the baseline into the proper service court. Use an overhand motion similar to the one used in baseball; people who are comfortable throwing a baseball learn to serve a tennis ball easily.

Variation: Throw to both deuce and ad courts.

Success Goal = 20 consecutive throws into the proper court

Your Score = (#) _____ throws

2. Service Toss Drill

Take a position behind the baseline and practice the service toss. Extend your fingers as you lift the ball, imparting as little spin as possible. Try to see the ball's seams during the toss. Let the ball drop to the court. It should hit the court a few inches inside the line in the direction of the diagonally opposite service court.

Success Goal = 10 good tosses out of 20 attempts

Your Score = (#) _____ tosses

3. Service Toss Target Drill

Draw a circle or place a racket cover at a point a few inches inside the baseline, where a correct toss would land if the ball were not hit. Count the number of times your tosses hit the target.

Follow the ball with your eyes until it hits the target. Keep your arm extended and away from your body.

Success Goal = 5 good tosses out of 10 attempts

Your Score = (#) _____ tosses

4. Net Post Toss Drill

Line up your tossing arm with the net post you are facing. Lift your arm in that direction, using the net post (or any other vertical point of reference) as a guide. Make your tossing arm follow that guide until you release the ball.

Success Goal = 10 consecutive tosses

Your Score = (#) _____ tosses

5. Service Line Serve Drill

Using the Keys to Success, practice serving into the proper courts from the service line instead of the baseline. Serve into the right and left courts. Bump the ball softly; don't blast the ball.

Success Goal = 7 accurate serves out of 10 attempts to both courts

Your Score = (#) _____ serves

6. Baseline Serve Drill

Practice serving into the proper courts from the baseline. Serve into both the right and left courts. Reach up—not forward—to strike the ball.

Success Goal = 5 good serves out of 10 attempts to both courts

Your Score = (#) _____ serves

7. Long Distance Serve Drill

Practice serving into the proper courts from a position 10 feet behind the baseline. The extra distance should make you stronger and more accurate once you move back up to the baseline.

Success Goal = 3 good serves out of 10 attempts to both courts

Your Score = (#) _____ serves

8. Punch Serve Target Drill

Place a cardboard box or similar target deep and in the middle of the service court. If you must make a mistake, it should be deep, not short.

Success Goal = 2 hits out of 10 attempts

Your Score = (#) _____ hits

9. Serve Return Game

Play a game with a partner, using only the serve and the service return. Every serve into the proper court counts 1 point, and every return counts 1 point. The server gets two chances to get the ball into play.

First player to score 10 points wins. Switch server and returner roles after each game. Concentrate on your serve—not on your opponent's return.

Success Goal = win at least half the games played

Your Score = (#) _____ wins, (#) _____ losses

Beginner's Serve
Keys to Success Checklist

Now that you have reached the Success Goals for the beginner's serve, ask a trained tennis observer to evaluate your technique according to the checklist below. Don't worry too much at this point about accuracy. Hold the racket with a forehand grip and stand at an angle to the baseline. Start with the racket behind your head, lift the ball higher than you can reach, then swing up at the ball. If you don't feel comfortable serving from the baseline, move forward to a point where you can get the ball into the proper service court. Then gradually serve from positions farther away from the net until you are back at the baseline position.

**Preparation
Phase**

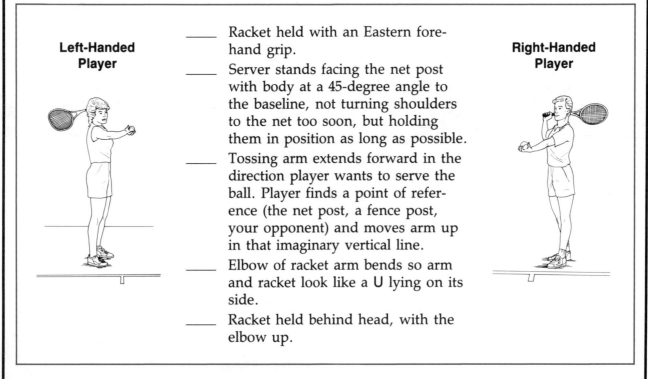

**Left-Handed
Player**

**Right-Handed
Player**

_____ Racket held with an Eastern forehand grip.

_____ Server stands facing the net post with body at a 45-degree angle to the baseline, not turning shoulders to the net too soon, but holding them in position as long as possible.

_____ Tossing arm extends forward in the direction player wants to serve the ball. Player finds a point of reference (the net post, a fence post, your opponent) and moves arm up in that imaginary vertical line.

_____ Elbow of racket arm bends so arm and racket look like a U lying on its side.

_____ Racket held behind head, with the elbow up.

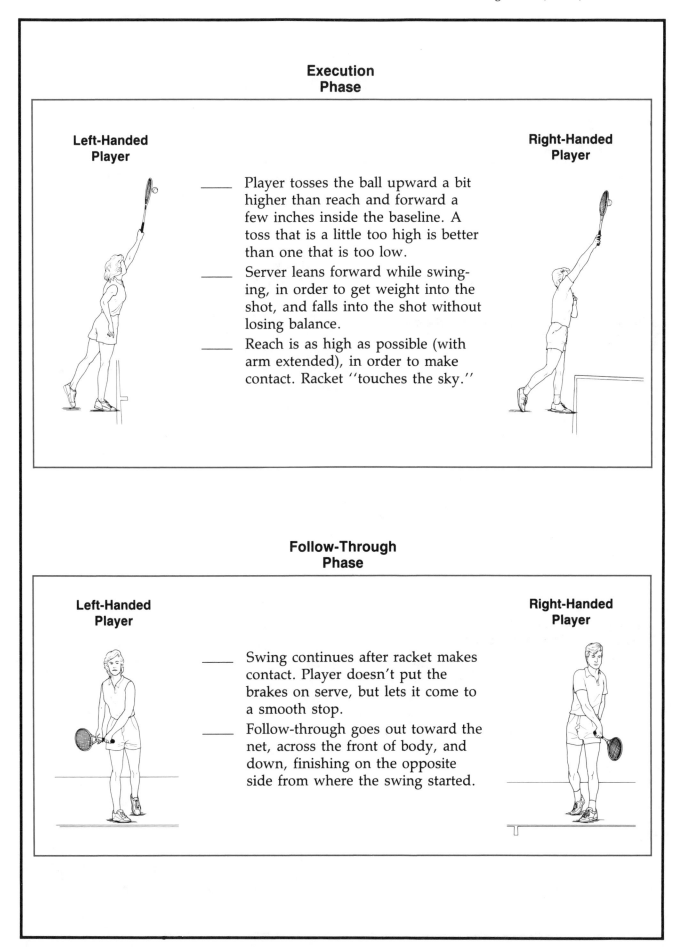

**Execution
Phase**

**Left-Handed
Player**

**Right-Handed
Player**

_____ Player tosses the ball upward a bit high than reach and forward a few inches inside the baseline. A toss that is a little too high is better than one that is too low.

_____ Server leans forward while swinging, in order to get weight into the shot, and falls into the shot without losing balance.

_____ Reach is as high as possible (with arm extended), in order to make contact. Racket "touches the sky."

**Follow-Through
Phase**

**Left-Handed
Player**

**Right-Handed
Player**

_____ Swing continues after racket makes contact. Player doesn't put the brakes on serve, but lets it come to a smooth stop.

_____ Follow-through goes out toward the net, across the front of body, and down, finishing on the opposite side from where the swing started.

Step 6   Full Swing Serve

The full swing serve allows you to move toward the intermediate and advanced levels of the game. It is called a *full swing* serve here because the motion is a complete preparation to hit the ball—not just the half-swing, punch method you practiced in Step 5. Instead of being only a device to get the point started, the full swing serve becomes an important item in your collection of strokes.

WHY IS THE FULL SWING SERVE IMPORTANT?

Breaking the serve means winning a game when your opponent is serving. At the intermediate and advanced levels of the game, *holding serve* (winning games when you are serving) becomes the primary objective in a match. If you always hold your serve and break the other player's serve only once during a set, you win. An effective serve becomes the key to winning because it means starting 50% of the points in a match with what should be an offensive shot. If your serve is weak, your opponent can attack it and has the chance to begin every point—your serve and his—on the attack.

HOW TO EXECUTE THE FULL SWING SERVE

Players with advanced serves usually hold the racket with a Continental grip. With it, the wrist is directly over the top of the racket handle as you look down over the top. Some players move their wrists a little toward the backhand side. These grips enable the player to serve with control, pace, and spin. The beginner's Eastern forehand grip for the serve is good mainly for control, although even a few advanced players use it with a full swing motion.

The position of your feet is very similar to the one described for the punch serve. Your side should be partially turned toward the net (remember the 45-degree angle) so you can twist into the ball with your swing. The angle at which you stand may vary a few degrees in either direction, depending on your individual preference.

Begin with your racket out in front of your body, pointing toward the target, about chest high, and with your nonracket hand holding the ball against the racket strings. As your racket head begins to drop in a pendulum motion by the side of your leg, the nonracket hand should also move slightly downward preliminary to the toss; both hands move down at the same time. The racket arm moves down, then into the back-scratching position while the other arm begins to move up to lift the ball for the toss. There should be a rhythmic feel to the serving motion.

You have to time the toss so that the ball reaches its highest point at the same time your hitting arm and racket extend to make contact. If the timing is not right, stop everything and start over. The toss also has to be far enough in front to force you to lean forward and beyond the baseline as you hit. Keep your head up and look at the ball while you are tossing.

As you bring the racket up and behind your back, your arm should begin to bend at the elbow and move through the back-scratching position. Fully extend your arm to make contact with the ball. When you serve, your body is almost in a straight line from the toes to the racket hand at the moment of impact.

To make the most of the weight transfer, your feet change position during the motion. As you lean forward, the foot closer to the line stays in the same place, but your other foot goes forward. Some players prefer to take one step, starting with the rear foot several inches from the baseline and finishing one step inside the line. Other players make a two-step approach with the rear foot. Bring your back foot forward to a point just behind the front foot prior to hitting. This movement results in a springboard effect into the service motion and may even give added height and leverage if you get up on your toes to hit. After you hit the ball, your foot continues forward, touching down one step inside the baseline. Regardless of the method you use, try to keep your knees slightly bent during the first part of the motion. As you hit, extending the knees adds to the springboard effect, giving you more power.

Follow through just like the beginners do. Reach out toward the net, then let your racket cross in front, finishing the stroke down and on the opposite side of your body.

In summary, the mechanics of the hitting phase of this serve are about the same as those you learned with the punch serve. The preparation is different and is made by developing a rhythmic momentum prior to striking the ball. Start with the ball on the racket strings with your arms extended in front of your body. Then your hands go down at the same time. Your tossing hand now goes up, while your racket arm bends at the elbow and accelerates upward to hit the ball when your arm extends (see Figure 6.1).

Figure 6.1   Keys to Success: Full Swing Serve

Preparation Phase

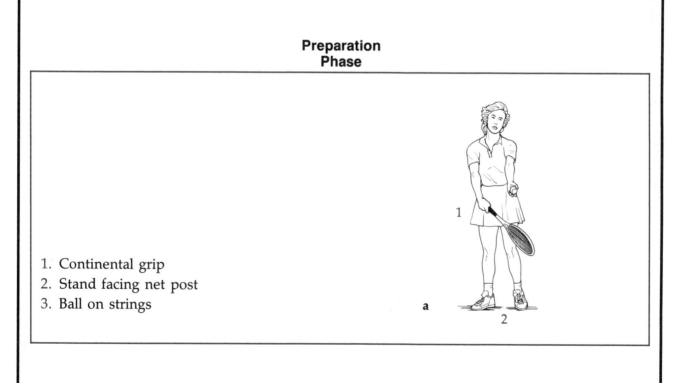

1. Continental grip
2. Stand facing net post
3. Ball on strings

**Execution
Phase**

1. Hands part going down
2. Hands up at same time
3. Lift ball upward, forward

4. Lean forward
5. Reach high to hit

**Follow-Through
Phase**

1. Continue swing after hit

2. Swing out, across, down

Detecting Errors in the Full Swing Serve

Mistakes on the serve cut across all levels of the game. Even world-class players toss too high or low, look out toward the court rather than up at the ball, don't transfer their weight forward, and do a few other things recreational players also do. This game is difficult to master, but correct stroke production is not as complicated as you think.

ERROR	CORRECTION
1. Your serve lacks power.	1. Develop more racket speed at the top of the swing. Move your weight forward with the swing; don't make your arm do all of the work.
2. You have a weak second serve.	2. Develop two medium-paced serves instead of one bullet and one floater. Accuracy is more important than speed.
3. There is general inconsistency.	3. If grip, stance, and pace check out, just give yourself more time to practice.
4. You serve into the net.	4. Do not let the ball drop too low before making contact; reach high to hit. Remember to follow through.
5. You serve too deep.	5. Check the grip. You may have slipped back to a forehand grip; stay with the Continental. Also, reduce the speed of your serve.

Full Swing Serve Drills

1. Racket Cover Serve Drill

Practice the service motion with the cover on the racket. The added weight and air resistance helps strengthen your serving arm. Make your elbow move upward with the swing.

Variation: Place additional lightweight objects inside the cover to increase the total weight.

Success Goal = 25 swings a day for 5 days

Your Score =

(#) _____ swings, day 1

(#) _____ swings, day 2

(#) _____ swings, day 3

(#) _____ swings, day 4

(#) _____ swings, day 5

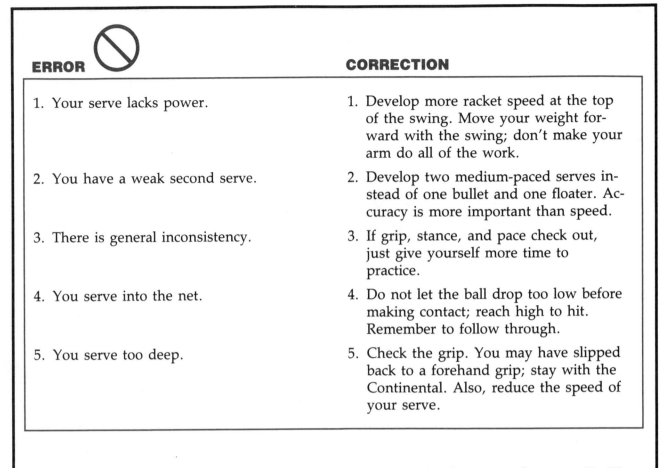

2. Serve Mirror Drill

Practice the full swing motion in front of a mirror in a room with a high ceiling. If this is not possible, practice the swing on a court, reaching as high as possible at the point of contact. Reach for the sky when you swing.

Success Goal = 25 service swings a day for 5 days

Your Score =

(#) _____ swings, day 1

(#) _____ swings, day 2

(#) _____ swings, day 3

(#) _____ swings, day 4

(#) _____ swings, day 5

3. Fence Serve Drill

If you have a limited number of balls, practice your service motion by serving into a fence from a distance of 15 feet. Select a real or imaginary point on the fence and try to hit it every time.

Success Goal = 25 serves a day for 5 days

Your Score =

(#) _____ serves, day 1

(#) _____ serves, day 2

(#) _____ serves, day 3

(#) _____ serves, day 4

(#) _____ serves, day 5

4. Consecutive Serve Drill

Count the number of consecutive balls served into both service courts, alternating courts as in a game. Work toward making your service motion so automatic that you don't even have to think about what you are doing.

Success Goal = 10 consecutive serves into both service courts

Your Score = (#) _____ serves

5. Target Serve Drill

Place a cardboard box or similar target in the backhand corners of the service court area (for right-handed receiver). Leave room for error; if your serve goes deeper than expected, it should still have a chance to be in.

Success Goal = 3 hits out of 10 serves

Your Score = (#) _____ target hits

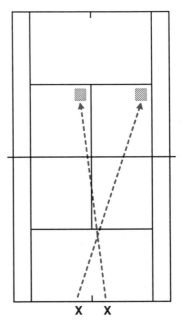

6. Serve and Return Games

Play a game with a partner, using only the serve and the service return. Every serve into the proper court counts 1 point, and every good return counts a point. The server gets two chances to get the ball in play. The first to score 10 points wins. Switch server and returner roles after each game. Remember—as server, your first priority is getting the serve in—not worrying about whether it will be returned.

Success Goal = win at least half the games played

Your Score = (#) _____ wins, (#) _____ losses

Full Swing Serve
Keys to Success Checklist

As you prepare for someone to observe and evaluate your full swing serve, work on developing a rhythmic serving motion. You have been playing tennis long enough now to start smoothing out the rough edges of your strokes. If your full swing motion is a series of jerky, unrelated steps, take more time to practice one continuous, flowing motion from the toss to the follow-through. Don't lose the momentum you have generated by stopping the motion in the middle of your swing. Get the parts of your body moving in a coordinated sequence that results in an efficient, strong, and accurate stroke. If you think you are ready, get an observer to check the points listed below. After each serve, verbalize your thoughts to your observer.

**Preparation
Phase**

_____ Racket held with a Continental grip. Player checks to see whether wrist is on top of the handle.

_____ Server stands facing the net post with body at a 45-degree angle to the baseline, and separates feet enough so weight can shift back, then forward.

_____ Serve motion starts with arms extended in front of body, hand holding the ball on the strings of the racket. Player deliberately plans what to do with the serve.

Execution Phase

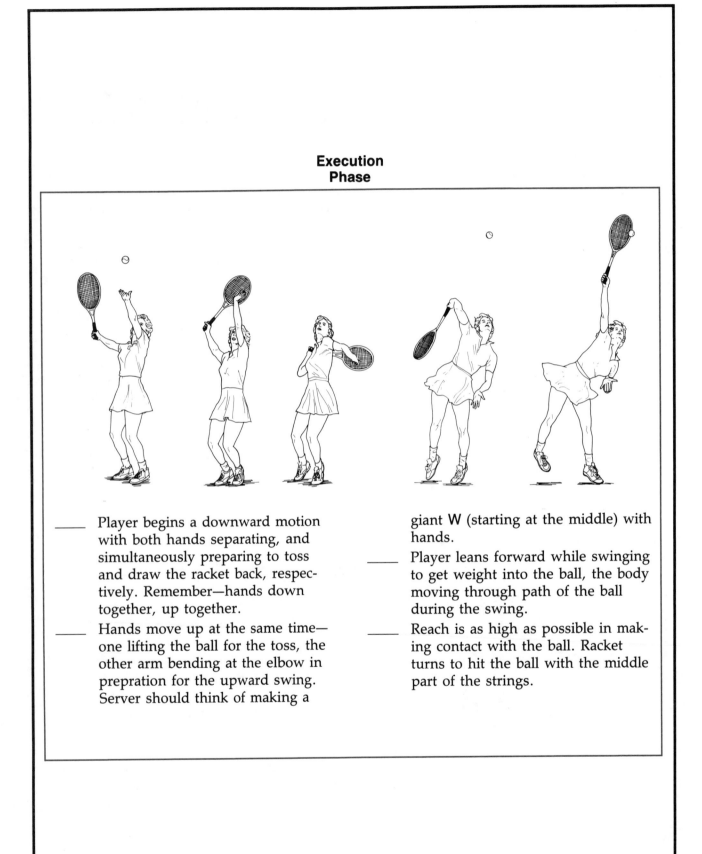

____ Player begins a downward motion with both hands separating, and simultaneously preparing to toss and draw the racket back, respectively. Remember—hands down together, up together.

____ Hands move up at the same time—one lifting the ball for the toss, the other arm bending at the elbow in prepration for the upward swing. Server should think of making a giant **W** (starting at the middle) with hands.

____ Player leans forward while swinging to get weight into the ball, the body moving through path of the ball during the swing.

____ Reach is as high as possible in making contact with the ball. Racket turns to hit the ball with the middle part of the strings.

Follow-Through
Phase

____ The swing continues after making contact with the ball. The serve does not start with contact, and it should not end at contact with the ball.

____ Swing goes out toward the net, across the front of body, and down, but not necessarily finishing on the opposite side. If back foot finishes the serve where it started, serve was performed incorrectly. The back foot should finish one step inside the baseline.

Step 7 Three-Shot Singles

Now you have three basic shots in your growing collection of strokes to start playing games, sets, and matches. With a serve, forehand, and backhand, you are ready to compete against another player, to keep score, and to see who wins and who loses. You are not ready for international competition, but you can start enjoying the same game that is played by millions of people around the world.

As you play, you will discover a few strengths and a lot of weaknesses. You will also accidentally hit some volleys, lobs, smashes, and other shots you have not learned or practiced. After playing a few games and sets, you will be ready to go back and further refine your three basic strokes and to learn new ones.

Play a set or a 2 out of 3-set match. Concentrate on keeping the ball in play and using the Keys to Success fundamentals. Don't worry about winning and losing. Just get out there, practice your strokes, get the scorekeeping routine down, and have a good time. There will be plenty of time to get serious later.

Answer the following questions in the spaces provided.

SCORING QUIZ

1. In no-ad scoring, how many points do you need to win a game?

2. In no-ad scoring, on which side does the server stand when the score is 3–2?

3. In no-ad scoring, on which side does the receiver stand when the score is 3–3?

4. In conventional scoring, what is the score if the server wins the first 2 points?

5. In conventional scoring, is the server or the receiver leading when the score is 30–40?

6. In conventional scoring, what is the score if the receiver wins the first 3 points?

7. In conventional scoring, what is the score if the server wins the first 3 points?

8. In conventional scoring, what is the score if the server wins the next point after each player had won 3 points?

9. In conventional scoring, what is the score if the server loses the point when the score was 40–30?

10. What does *ad in* mean?

11. What does *ad out* mean?

12. What is the fewest number of points possible in a game?

13. What is the fewest number of games possible in a set?

14. In a pro set, how many games must be won to win the set?

15. What is the least number of points that must be won to win a tiebreaker?

16. Who serves first in a tiebreaker?

17. Where does the server stand on the first point of a tiebreaker?

18. From which sides, in order, are the second and third points of a tiebreaker served?

19. When do players change ends of the court during a tiebreaker?

20. Do players change ends of the court immediately after a tiebreaker, before the next set begins?

ANSWERS TO SCORING QUIZ

1. 4
2. Left, facing the net
3. The receiver has the option.
4. 30-0
5. The receiver
6. 0-40
7. 40-0
8. Ad in (advantage server)
9. Deuce
10. The server has the advantage; if he (she) wins the next point, the game is over.
11. The receiver has the advantage; if he (she) wins the next point, the game is over.
12. 4
13. 6
14. 8
15. 7
16. The player who would have served the next game
17. The right side, facing the net
18. Left side, then right side
19. After every 6 points that have been played
20. Yes

Singles and Scoring Drills

1. No-Ad Games

Play 2 out of 3 games, 3 out of 5 games, or 1 set using no-ad scoring. Remember—The first player to win 4 points wins the game. Also, if the score is 3–3 in a game, the receiver has the option of receiving the serve from either the left or right side.

Success Goal = play 2 out of 3 or 3 out of 5 games

Your Score = (#) _____ games played

2. Deuce Games

Play a set in which every game starts with the score at deuce. If weather conditions are not a factor, change sides of the court only once—after you have completed 5 games. Spin a racket to determine serve and side.

Success Goal = play a set

Your Score = (#) _____ games played

3. Sets

Play 1 set, or 2 out of 3 sets, using conventional scoring. Remember to spin a racket to determine serve and side. Also remember to change ends of the court every time the total number of games played is an odd number.

Success Goal = play a set or 2 out of 3 sets

Your Score = (#) _____ sets played

4. Finishing Sets

Play 1 set or 2 out of 3 sets, starting with the score at 4–4 in each set. Spin the racket to determine serve and side. With the score starting at 4–4, every point is crucial. Learn to play under pressure.

Success Goal = play a set or 2 out of 3 sets

Your Score = (#) _____ sets played

5. Tiebreaker Drill

Play 2 out of 3 tiebreakers. Learning to keep score and to serve and receive in tiebreakers is difficult, but becomes easier with repetition. Try to win, but the main objective is to go through the process several times to learn how it works. Worry about winning later.

Success Goal = play 2 out of 3 tiebreakers

Your Score = (#) _____ tiebreakers won, (#) _____ tiebreakers lost

Step 8   Beginner's Volley

The *volley* is a shot hit before the ball bounces on your side of the court. Although it is usually hit in the forecourt area, it might be used anywhere on the court. There are fewer fundamental skills to master in a volley, but there is less time to prepare and execute the shot, because you are standing closer to the net. The only difference between the beginner's volley and that of an advanced player is the grip.

WHY IS THE VOLLEY IMPORTANT?

There are two reasons for being in a position to hit a volley. The first is that you have moved toward the net to return a shot hit by your opponent and have no choice about the next shot. The second reason is that you are playing aggressively and want to end a point by putting the ball away (out of your opponent's reach) from an attacking position near the net. In either case, the technique of hitting the volley is different from that of groundstrokes. Learning it is a necessary part of your development as a player.

HOW TO EXECUTE THE BEGINNER'S VOLLEY

Unlike hitting groundstrokes, hitting volleys correctly is not a very natural motion. Because you are close to the net, there is no time for much of a backswing. For the time being, use a forehand grip for forehand shots and a backhand grip for backhand shots; this will change later. The swing is one of a block or a punch, and the pace on the ball comes from your body's movement forward.

Stand in the ready position 8–10 feet from the net. Move in even closer if you are hitting volleys for the first time. Keep your racket directly in front of your body, with your arms extended. You should have your racket in a position exactly halfway between your forehand and backhand sides. Your weight should be forward so your heels are barely in touch with the court, if in contact at all. Bend your knees enough to get the feeling of hitting out of a crouch. Bend slightly forward at your waist. As the ball approaches, you want to be in a position to spring out for the shot.

If the ball comes to your right side, use your right foot to pivot, and step forward in the direction you want to hit with your left foot. Concentrate on moving forward instead of moving laterally along the net or pivoting in reverse. If the ball comes to your left side, pivot on your left foot, and step across and into the ball with your right foot. If the ball comes directly at you, slide to one side of the path of the ball by pushing off with one foot and stepping at an angle toward the net with the other.

The backswing on either side is a short, restricted motion. As you see the ball coming, bring the racket back to a point not much farther than an imaginary line even with your back and parallel to the net. If an observer were to stand on the side opposite your racket hand, your racket should not be visible.

Throughout the entire motion, keep your wrist locked so that the racket forms a nearly 90-degree angle with your forearm. Lead the stroke with the racket head. Swing forward from your shoulder, not your wrist or elbow. Make contact well in front of your body. Try to hit the ball while it is rising. Attack it, rather than let it get even with or behind you.

If you have stepped forward, your weight should be on the foot closer to the net. The shoulder closer to the net should be down. Direct your volleys deep into the backcourt or at an angle to pull the other player off the court.

Remember—racket out in front while waiting, weight forward, short backswing, and hit the ball before it gets even with you. Follow through in the direction you want to hit, but recover quickly for the next shot (see Figures 8.1 and 8.2).

To be extra alert, many players crouch low and bounce on the balls of their feet when they expect a shot to be hit right at them. If the shot comes low, do not stand straight up and put the racket down to hit the ball; bend your knees even more and get down to eye level with the ball. The angle of the racket on a low volley is the same as on any other volley because you are bending your knees instead of bending at your waist or dropping the racket head. Avoid volleying up on the ball. If you volley up, your opponent will be in a position to hit down for a possible winner on the return.

Figure 8.1 Keys to Success: Beginner's Forehand Volley

Preparation Phase

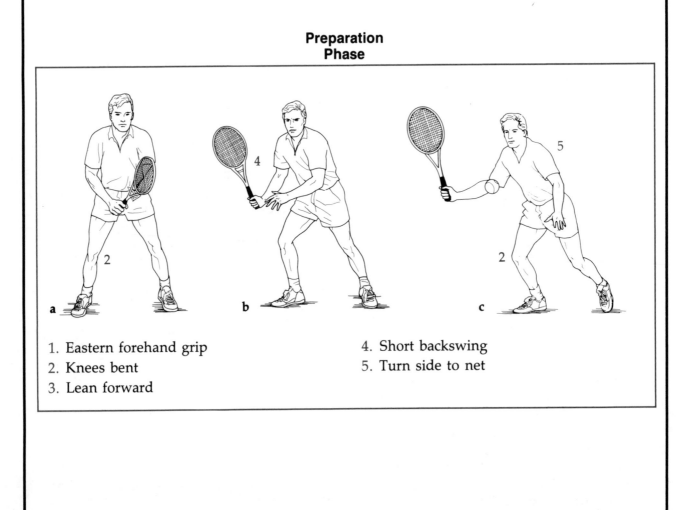

1. Eastern forehand grip
2. Knees bent
3. Lean forward
4. Short backswing
5. Turn side to net

Execution
Phase

d

e

1. Forward with opposite foot
2. Reach forward to hit
3. Make contact at side

4. Tight grip at contact
5. Eyes level with ball

Follow-Through
Phase

f

1. Shorter swing after hit
2. Recover for next shot

Figure 8.2 Keys to Success:
**Beginner's
Backhand Volley**

**Preparation
Phase**

1. Eastern backhand grip
2. Knees bent
3. Lean forward

4. Short backswing
5. Turn side to net

**Execution
Phase**

1. Forward with opposite foot
2. Reach forward to hit
3. Make a contact at side

4. Tight grip at contact
5. Eyes level with ball

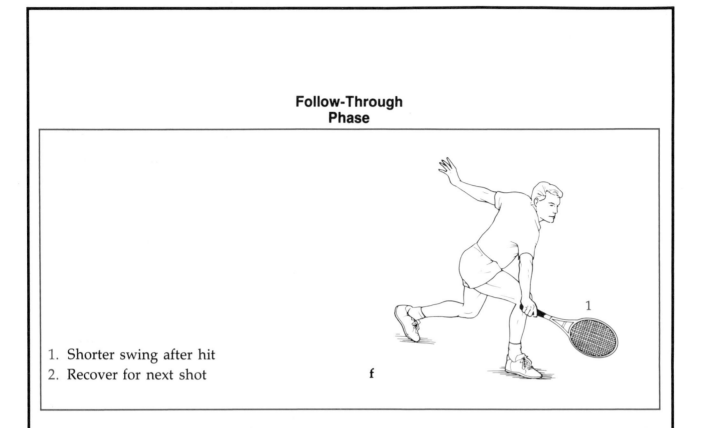

**Follow-Through
Phase**

1. Shorter swing after hit
2. Recover for next shot

f

HOW TO USE THE
BEGINNER'S VOLLEY IN SINGLES

Have a reason for going to the net. The best reason is that you have hit a deep or wide forcing shot, putting your opponent in trouble. Then it is a good situation for you to move forward and take charge of the point. Whatever you do, don't hit an average shot that will take one bounce and go to your opponent's forehand; you would be asking to be passed with an easy groundstroke.

Once you have hit a shot you can follow by moving to the net, just try to volley your opponent's return to the open spot on the court or to your opponent's weakness. Just as football players ''run to daylight,'' tennis players should automatically hit where the other player is not. This frequently means hitting crosscourt volleys, but there are many exceptions, such as when your opponent is anticipating the crosscourt volley and has already started to move in the right direction. Then you can hit the volley down the line or down the middle in anticipation of where the open spot on the court will soon be.

Remember that volleys do not have to be hit near the lines to be winners. If the first volley is not good enough to be a winning shot, the second volley should be. Move in closer to the net after a strong volley; hold your ground and hope for the best if you hit a weak one. If you stay at the net more than 3 consecutive volleys, the chances of your winning the point are not very good.

Detecting Errors in the Beginner's Volley

Some players are intimidated by opponents who hit hard, and others are discouraged from going to the net if they are not successful early in their volleying experience. Knowing the most common volley errors and some suggestions for correcting those errors may make you feel better about hitting volleys.

ERROR 🚫

CORRECTION

ERROR	CORRECTION
1. Your volley lacks power.	1. Step forward to move your body's weight into the shot.
2. You hit late.	2. Take a short backswing. Otherwise, while you are winding up, the ball will get past you.
3. Racket turns in hand at impact.	3. Hold the racket tighter than on groundstrokes; the ball gets to you sooner and with more pace than at the baseline.
4. You volley into the net.	4. Play close to the net until your skills improve. Keep your eyes at ball level and your wrist in a cocked position. Do not try to hit down on the ball; just make contact and bump it up or straight back. Open the racket face to the sky slightly, and hit "through" the ball.

Beginner's Volley Drills

1. *Mirror Volley Drill*

Watch yourself swing through forehand and backhand volleys in a mirror. Remember to look for one component of the swing at a time (footwork, grip, or swinging motion, for instance).

Success Goal = 25 forehand and 25 backhand volley swings

Your Score =

    (#) _____ forehand volley swings

    (#) _____ backhand volley swings

2. *Racket Catch Drill*

Have a partner stand at a distance of about 20 feet and toss balls to both your forehand and backhand sides. Instead of hitting volleys, simply put the racket strings in front of the ball as if to catch it.

    You have worked on this type of drill in Step 3, but there you were catching the ball after the bounce. Now stop the ball with your racket strings (not the frame) before it bounces. Notice how much of the work the racket and strings do by themselves.

Success Goal = 20 consecutive string catches

Your Score = (#) _____ string catches

3. Toss to Volley Drill

Have a partner stand at a distance of 20 feet on the other side of the net and toss balls first to your forehand side, then to your backhand. Direct your volleys anywhere in the singles court on the opposite side of the net.

Don't wait for the ball to come to you. Go forward by taking a step with your opposite foot to get to the ball rather than waiting for it to come to where you are.

Variation: Return tosses with volleys that your partner can catch or reach with at least one hand. The idea is to practice controlled volleys and not to have to chase balls every 3 shots. If you can learn to hit to a target, you can also learn to hit away from it.

Success Goal = 10 volleys out of 15 tosses, to each side

Your Score =

(#) _____ volleys on forehand side

(#) _____ volleys on backhand side

4. Back-to-the-Wall Volley Drill

Stand with your back against a fence or wall and return volleys tossed by a partner. Volley without your racket touching the fence or wall on the backswing; get into the habit of moving forward to hit volleys.

Variation: Volley without touching the wall and so accurately that the tosser can catch or reach your shot with at least one hand.

Success Goal = 20 consecutive volleys without touching the wall or fence

Your Score = (#) _____ volleys

5. Consecutive Volley Drill

Keep the ball in play hitting only volleys with a partner, who may hit volleys or ground-strokes. This is a difficult drill, even for intermediate players. It works better if your partner is an intermediate or advanced player. If your practice partner is at the baseline, work on getting your volleys deep into the backcourt.

 Don't try to win points yet; just get used to the idea that not only can you play at the net, you can also place the ball where you want it to go. Later, you can begin hitting volleys with pace, depth, and purpose.

Variation: Volley against two players on the baseline, alternating volleys to each.

Success Goal = 20 consecutive volleys hit into the opposite singles court

Your Score = (#) _____ volleys

Beginner's Volley Keys to Success Checklist

In Step 8, the emphasis is on efficiency and quickness rather than on sweeping strokes that take time for preparation and execution. Remember that when you are at the net, you do not have as much time as you would like. Anticipate trouble when you play at the net. Expect every shot to come right at you. Think ahead about what you are going to do if every shot actually does come in your direction. When you do hit volleys, do it with a short, compact stroke. Get power by leaning forward or stepping in the direction you want the ball to go. The observer will watch for a forehand or backhand grip, a short backswing, side to the net, forward movement, early contact, eyes level with the ball, and a quick recovery after the shot. Good luck!

Preparation Phase

Beginner's Forehand Volley

Beginner's Backhand Volley

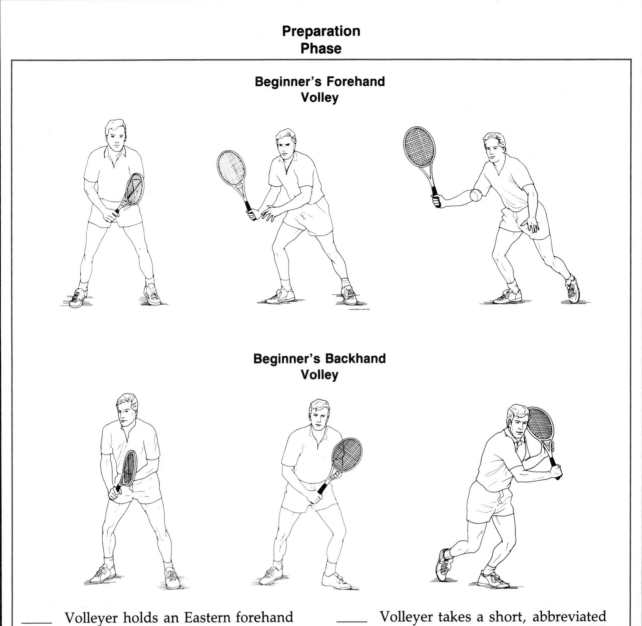

_____ Volleyer holds an Eastern forehand grip on the forehand side, then changes to an Eastern backhand for backhand volleys. A beginner has the luxury of changing grips. An intermediate or advanced player learns to hold the same grip for forehand and backhand volleys.

_____ Player bends knees and leans forward so that heels are slightly off the ground, expecting trouble. Every ball could come hard and directly at the player. A player should be prepared for the worst, and everything else will be a pleasant surprise.

_____ Volleyer takes a short, abbreviated backswing (2 feet or less). The bigger the windup, the quicker the ball will get past the player. Ask player to "imagine someone behind you trying to interfere with your swing, and get your racket out of the way before it happens."

_____ When there is time, side opposite from the racket hand turns toward the net. If there's not time to take a step, player at least turns shoulders.

Execution Phase

Beginner's Forehand Volley

Beginner's Backhand Volley

_____ Volleyer steps forward while hitting, in order to get power with shot. Because there is not a lot of power from the swing, the player must get his or her body into the shot.

_____ Contact made out in front of body (before the ball gets even with it) and out to the side of where player is standing. A player should not ever let a shot come directly at the face. If it does, he or she needs to step to one side and put racket where face used to be.

_____ Volleyer tightens grip while making contact to prevent the racket from turning in hand. The ball gets to the player sooner and harder than when at the baseline, so a tight grip is needed to handle the force of the ball. Player can relax grip a bit between shots.

_____ Eyes stay level with the ball, player getting down for low shots instead of shooting from the hip. Like shooting a pistol, the player will be more accurate if eyes are lined up with weapon and target.

**Follow-Through
Phase**

**Beginner's Forehand
Volley**

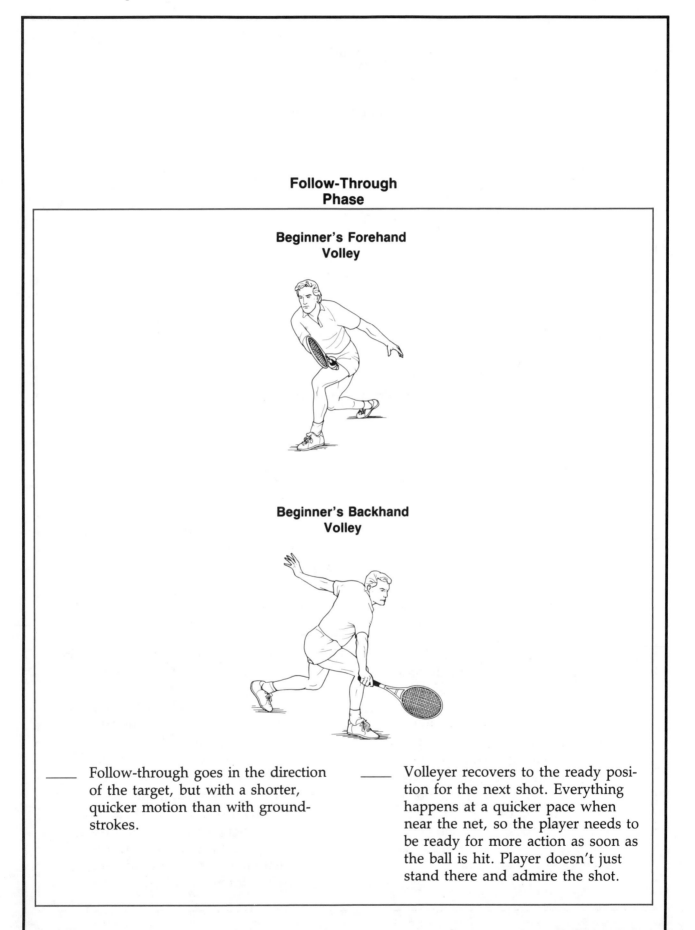

**Beginner's Backhand
Volley**

_____ Follow-through goes in the direction of the target, but with a shorter, quicker motion than with ground-strokes.

_____ Volleyer recovers to the ready position for the next shot. Everything happens at a quicker pace when near the net, so the player needs to be ready for more action as soon as the ball is hit. Player doesn't just stand there and admire the shot.

Step 9 Lob

The lob is one of the game's most valuable shots, but one that players seldom take time to practice or refine. The *lob* is a high, arching shot with fundamentals not very different from a forehand or backhand groundstroke. It simply goes higher, softer, and deeper into the backcourt than most groundstrokes.

WHY IS THE LOB IMPORTANT?

This shot is effective as an offensive weapon, as a defensive technique, and as a way to keep your opponent off-balance. The lob is not something you use only when you are in trouble; you should use it any time it can help you win a point—this is more often than most players realize. Try it occasionally, even if it costs a point; it will give your opponent something else to think about. If there is never any threat of a lob, the other player can always anticipate that you are going to drive the ball with normal groundstrokes.

HOW TO EXECUTE THE LOB

Hold the racket as you would for any groundstroke; there is no special grip for the lob. If a shot comes to your forehand side, use the forehand grip you have been practicing for groundstrokes. Change to the Eastern or two-handed backhand for lobs on the opposite side of your body.

The offensive lob is designed to win the point by being a shot your opponent does not expect. For example, the other player has hit an average forehand or backhand stroke and has come to the net behind that shot. In most cases, you would try to hit a *passing shot* (one that passes the other player at the net). Since you know this shot might be anticipated, an offensive lob would catch him or her off-guard and go overhead for a winner.

Make your preparation look like that for any other shot in your groundstroke collection. If you give the preparation a different look, the other player will anticipate what you are up to and get into a position to smash your lob.

Just before you make contact with the ball, rotate your wrist so that the racket face opens slightly to the sky. Although some advanced players occasionally hit a topspin lob, most of the time the shot is hit flat (without spin) or with backspin. The opened racket face allows for backspin. The point of contact may be farther back in relationship to your body than on other shots because you are probably returning a forcing shot and because if you can wait another fraction of a second, your opponent will be committed even farther toward the net.

With the open face, lift the ball upward and aim it high enough to clear your opponent's outstretched racket. You should hit the ball high enough so that it cannot be reached before the bounce and low enough so it cannot be reached after the bounce. Direct the ball to the backhand side whenever possible. If you make a mistake, make it by hitting too high or too deep—not by hitting too low or too short, where your opponent could easily put it away.

Follow through in the direction you are attempting to hit the ball. The follow-through may not be as complete as on normal groundstrokes, but do not deliberately restrict this part of the stroke. Hold your racket firmly, keep your wrist steady, and try to carry the ball on the strings as long as possible. If you think too much of shortening the follow-through, you may begin to slow down the racket before contact. If that happens, the lob would fall short.

Just as when hitting offensive lobs, hitting defensive lobs does not require a special grip. You may have to hold the racket tighter to withstand the force of an opponent's smash, but hold either a backhand or forehand grip as you would for other groundstrokes.

When you hit a defensive lob you are probably either running, out of position, off-balance, or generally in trouble. Technique is not quite as important when you are scrambling to stay alive in a rally, but technique should not be overlooked entirely. Anytime you are in trouble on the tennis court, shorten your swing. There are times when the motion you use in returning a smash or any other hard-hit shot looks almost like a volley motion. Take a short backswing when you hit a defensive lob. If the other player has hit the ball hard enough, you may be able just to block the ball upward to get it back.

Again, the racket face is open a bit as you make contact. Lift the ball; get it well into the air so you have enough time to recover and get back into position for the next shot. If your opponent's smash was hard enough, you may

not have to lift the ball to get it back; just getting your racket on the ball in time and opening the face may be enough to send the ball back high and deep.

If you can, follow through, but don't worry about it unless you are having problems. The follow-through is upward, outward, and across your body, in that order. A full follow-through helps you get the feel of gently lifting the ball into the air and deep into the backcourt. However, if you are really in trouble, get the ball back any way you can to survive the point.

See Figures 9.1 and 9.2 for the Keys to Success for the forehand lob and the backhand lob.

Figure 9.1 Keys to Success: Forehand Lob

Preparation Phase

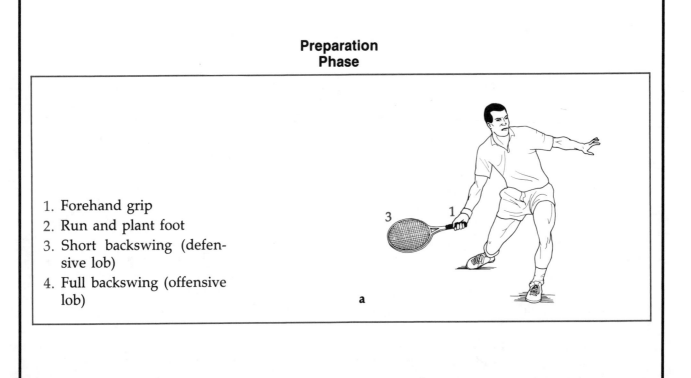

1. Forehand grip
2. Run and plant foot
3. Short backswing (defensive lob)
4. Full backswing (offensive lob)

Execution
Phase

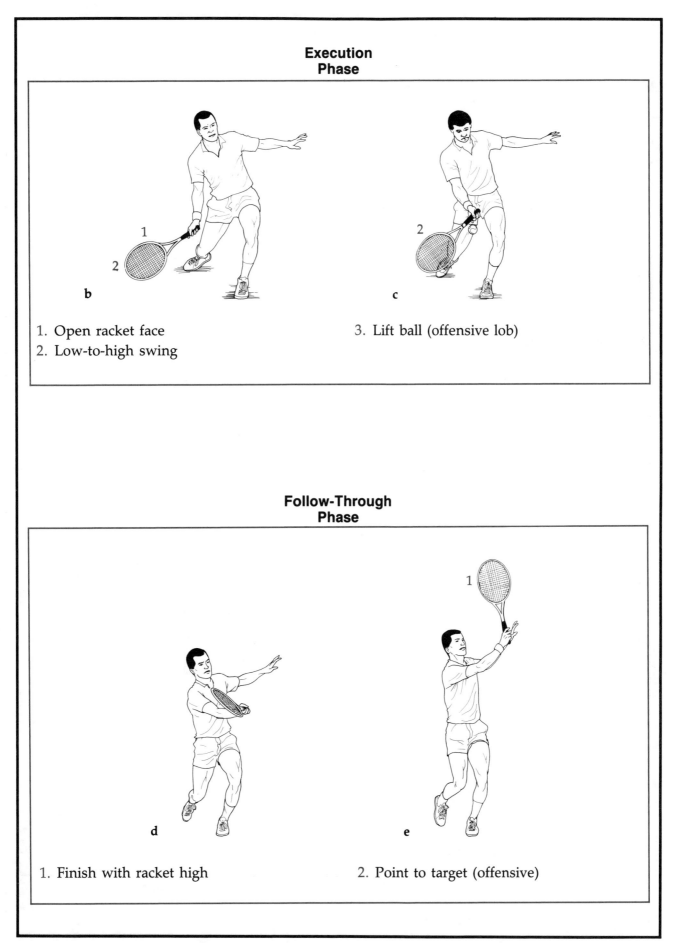

b

1. Open racket face
2. Low-to-high swing

3. Lift ball (offensive lob)

c

Follow-Through
Phase

d

e

1. Finish with racket high

2. Point to target (offensive)

Figure 9.2 Keys to Success:
Backhand Lob

**Preparation
Phase**

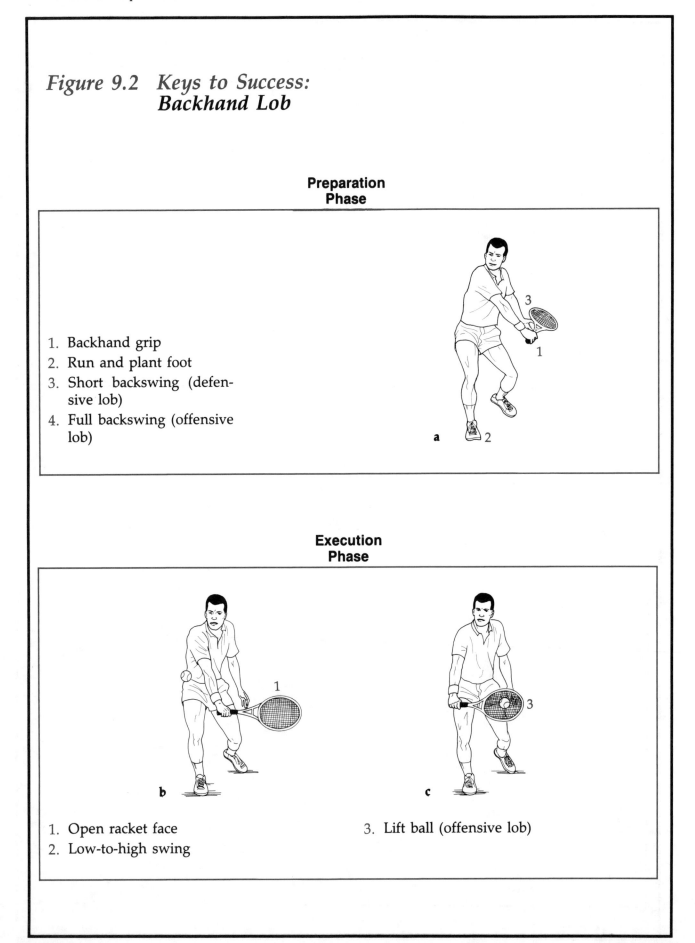

1. Backhand grip
2. Run and plant foot
3. Short backswing (defensive lob)
4. Full backswing (offensive lob)

**Execution
Phase**

1. Open racket face
2. Low-to-high swing

3. Lift ball (offensive lob)

**Follow-Through
Phase**

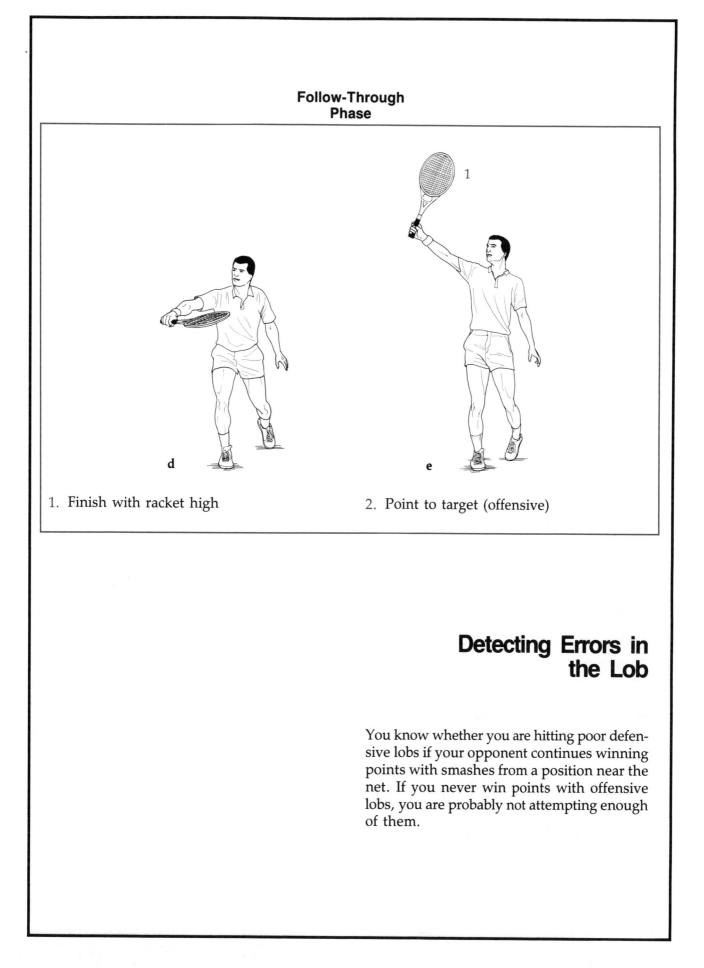

1. Finish with racket high

2. Point to target (offensive)

Detecting Errors in the Lob

You know whether you are hitting poor defensive lobs if your opponent continues winning points with smashes from a position near the net. If you never win points with offensive lobs, you are probably not attempting enough of them.

ERROR	CORRECTION
1. You lob too short.	1. Aim for the back third of the court. Any errors should be deep, not short.
2. You lob too deep.	2. Reduce the size of your backswing; the pace of your opponent's shot can be reflected back without too much effort. Check the angle of the racket face at contact.

Lob Drills

1. Drop-and-Hit Lob Drill

Standing behind the baseline, drop the ball and hit forehand lobs into the opposite court. Aim for specific areas in the backcourt, such as the forehand or backhand corners between the service line and the baseline. Use a full backswing and follow-through in this drill.

Variation: Lob over a partner standing at the service line and holding the racket up as high as possible. Every lob should clear your partner's racket and land inside the baseline.

Success Goal = 10 of 15 attempts hitting in the opponent's backcourt

Your Score = (#) _____ attempts

2. Run and Lob Drill

Have a partner stand at the net and alternately drive shots to your forehand and backhand corners. Move to the ball and return the shots with lobs.

Take short steps to get started, then put your engine in high gear as you run toward the ball. Don't worry as much about technique as just managing to chase the ball down and stay in the point one more shot.

Variation: Play the point out after the lob.

Success Goal = 10 of 20 shots with a lob that hits in the opponent's backcourt

Your Score = (#) _____ lobs

Lob
Keys to Success Checklist

This is a shot that is relatively easy to hit in practice or drill situations, but rather difficult when someone is standing at the net ready to hit an overhead smash if you make a mistake. Before a teacher or coach evaluates your technique, it may be a good idea to practice with a friend who actually smashes your short lobs. Most tennis teachers will be a little more lenient about technique with this stroke than with others. What matters is whether or not you can execute the shot—not whether you look good doing it. However, if you are having trouble with this stroke, your teacher, coach, or another trained observer may be able to help identify the problem by checking the following items.

**Preparation
Phase**

**Forehand
Lob**

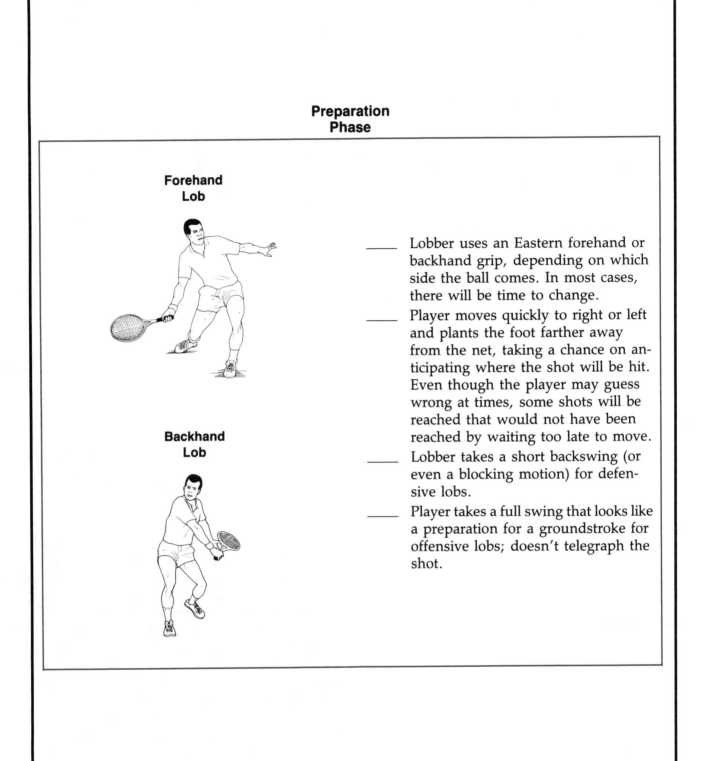

**Backhand
Lob**

_____ Lobber uses an Eastern forehand or backhand grip, depending on which side the ball comes. In most cases, there will be time to change.

_____ Player moves quickly to right or left and plants the foot farther away from the net, taking a chance on anticipating where the shot will be hit. Even though the player may guess wrong at times, some shots will be reached that would not have been reached by waiting too late to move.

_____ Lobber takes a short backswing (or even a blocking motion) for defensive lobs.

_____ Player takes a full swing that looks like a preparation for a groundstroke for offensive lobs; doesn't telegraph the shot.

Execution
Phase

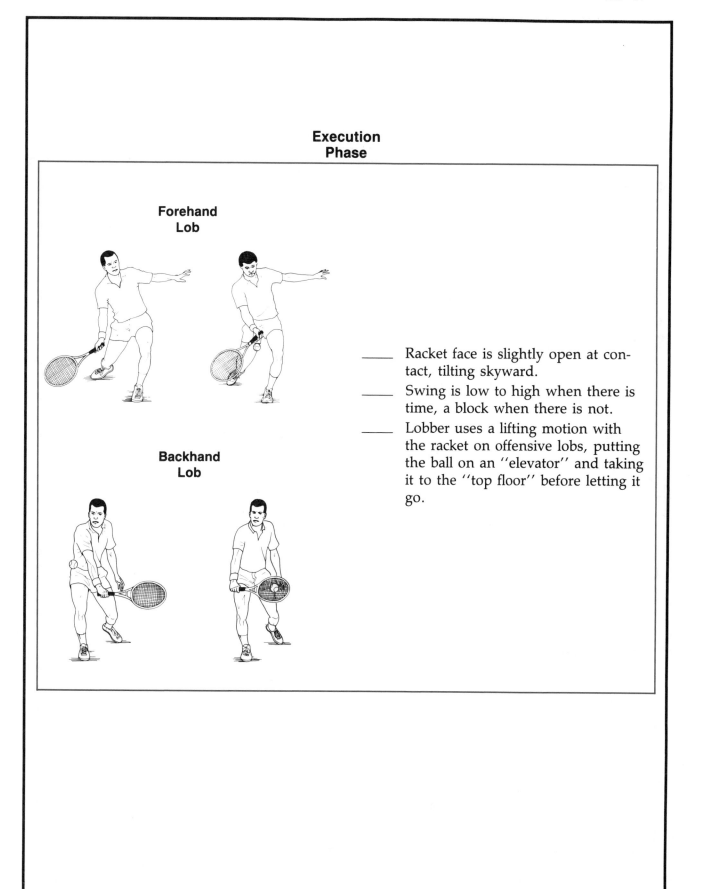

**Forehand
Lob**

**Backhand
Lob**

_____ Racket face is slightly open at contact, tilting skyward.

_____ Swing is low to high when there is time, a block when there is not.

_____ Lobber uses a lifting motion with the racket on offensive lobs, putting the ball on an "elevator" and taking it to the "top floor" before letting it go.

Follow-Through Phase

Forehand Lob

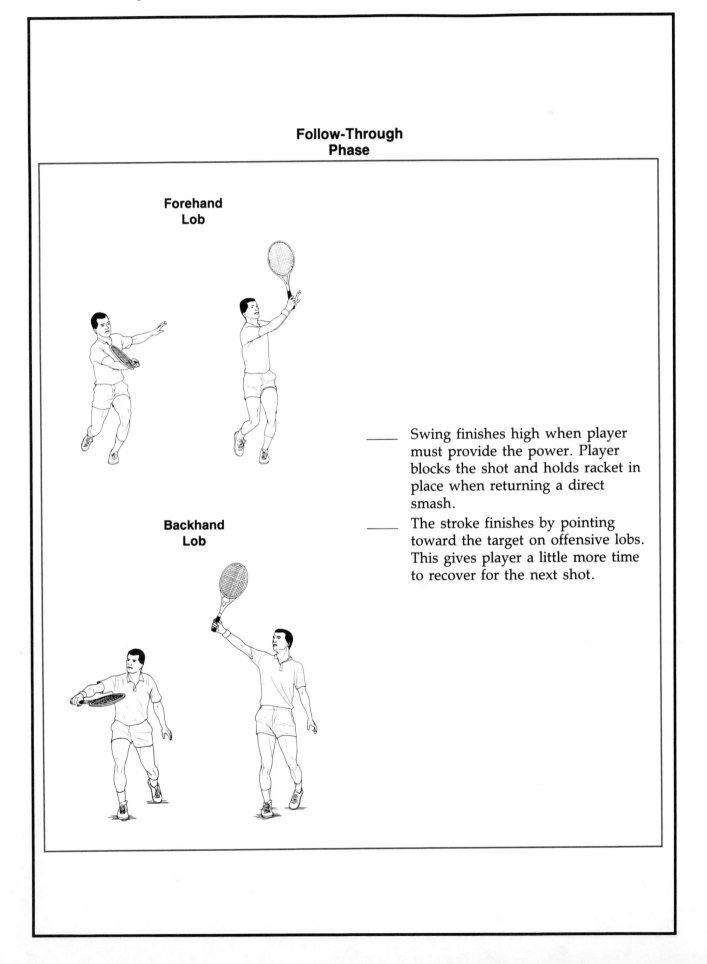

Backhand Lob

_____ Swing finishes high when player must provide the power. Player blocks the shot and holds racket in place when returning a direct smash.

_____ The stroke finishes by pointing toward the target on offensive lobs. This gives player a little more time to recover for the next shot.

Step 10   Smash

The *overhead smash* is an aggressive, offensive, hard shot you usually hit from the forecourt area after your opponent has tried to lob the ball over your head. If you are in an offensive position, it can be a powerful, point-ending shot. Some of the fundamentals of the smash are similar to those of the serve, so when you practice one of these two shots, you are also working on the other.

WHY IS THE SMASH IMPORTANT?

If your opponent knows you have a weak overhead smash, he or she will try to get you to come to the net, and then will exploit your weakness. A good smash makes you a more intimidating opponent and offers another way for you to win points. It is one of the few shots in tennis in which you can let go and try for an all-out winner. A good smash can have a demoralizing effect on the other player, which may help you win subsequent points.

HOW TO EXECUTE THE SMASH

Beginners and some intermediate players may have to hold the racket with a forehand grip with this shot, but as you get better, start changing to the Continental grip. Use this grip if you can on the smash for the same reason advanced players use it on the serve: It allows you to snap your wrist at the top of the swing, and it gives you some alternatives about what to do with the ball.

Because this grip is similar to the one you use to hit a backhand, and because you hit the smash on the forehand side of you body, you have to make some adjustments. The main adjustment is rotating your wrist outward just before contact. An outward rotation means that looking at the back of your hand, your thumb goes away from you, down, and across. This *pronation* type of movement allows you to hit the ball flat and with more force than

you put on groundstrokes. The inward and downward snap of your thumb and forearm puts added zip on the ball. If you did not rotate your wrist, the shot would have too much spin and would probably go off too far to the side; also, the ball would move with less velocity, which is bad for a smash.

Take lots of steps to get ready. Not moving the feet during preparation is one of the most common errors made by players at all levels. Too many players see a lob coming, dig into a fixed position with both feet, then try to hit. The problem is that because lobs are in the air longer than other shots, variables such as velocity, spin, and trajectory may change during the flight of the ball. If you get set too soon, you might misread some of the variables and not make the right adjustments. Take several short half-steps and quarter-steps while preparing to hit. Active feet help you be in the perfect position to hit when the time comes.

As soon as you see that you can hit a smash, turn your side to the net so that one foot is forward and one back (as in the serve). Right-handers, put your right foot back and your left one forward; left-handers, do just the opposite. As you hit, push off with your back foot and transfer your weight forward.

Bring the racket directly up in front of your body and to a position behind your head as you prepare to hit. If you were to take a full swing, you would drop the racket down and bring it up behind your back in the pendulum and back-scratch motion. By eliminating the full swing, you can reduce the margin of error. If your position on the court is good enough, you still have enough power to put the ball away or hit a well-placed shot. The full backswing can give a more powerful motion, but it is less efficient and less accurate here than the restricted backswing.

As you draw the racket up behind your head, you might point to the ball with your opposite hand. Pointing can improve concentration and make you aware of your position in relation to the ball, but it may be difficult if you're a beginning player. Use the pointing technique only if it helps you hit better smashes; it is not an essential fundamental for this stroke.

The smashing motion is similar to a forceful punch serve. Bring your racket forward as if throwing it across the net, and reach as high as you can to make contact. As you swing, make your weight move into the ball. Hit the ball at a point in front of your body. As you hit, rotate your wrist outward and snap down with the thumb. If you are close to the net, hit the ball with as little spin as you can to get maximum velocity. If you are at midcourt, use some spin to make the ball curve down and into the court. If you are in the backcourt, put even more spin on the shot because the distance between you and your opponent is too far for a flat shot to be effective.

Follow through down and across your body. Bring the racket through the stroke naturally, then return it to the ready position for the next shot (see Figure 10.1).

Figure 10.1 Keys to Success: Smash

Preparation Phase

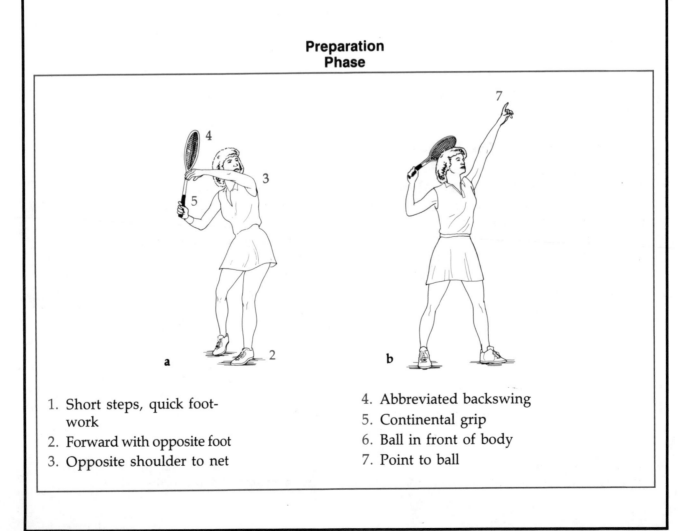

1. Short steps, quick footwork
2. Forward with opposite foot
3. Opposite shoulder to net
4. Abbreviated backswing
5. Continental grip
6. Ball in front of body
7. Point to ball

Execution
Phase

1. Reach high to hit
2. Flat hit—no spin

c

Follow-Through
Phase

1. Continue swing after hit
2. Racket away, across, down
3. Return to ready position

d

Detecting Errors in the Smash

Learning to recognize and execute a smash is easier if you can compare both correct and incorrect techniques. The most common overhead smash errors are listed below, along with suggestions on how to correct them.

ERROR

CORRECTION

ERROR	CORRECTION
1. Your smash goes beyond the baseline.	1. Maintain the Continental grip; inexperienced players slip back to a forehand grip without knowing it.
2. You mis-hit the ball.	2. Keep your head up throughout the swing; try to see yourself make contact with the ball. Restrict the backswing; too much movement causes errors.
3. Your smash lacks power.	3. Making contact late (behind your head) and a lack of racket speed at contact both cause weak shots. Also, you might point at the ball with the opposite hand, then try to make contact where you are pointing.
4. You hit into the net.	4. Do not let the ball drop too low. Reach up to hit with your arm extended.

Smash Drills

1. Shadow Smash Drill

Take a position at the net and swing through the overhead smash motion without hitting a ball. Turn, draw the racket straight back, and reach high as you swing. Repeat the sequence 10 times.

Variation: Stand close enough to the net to slap it with your racket as you follow through. Make contact with the net by hitting it flat, the entire face of the racket coming down on the top of the net to make a popping sound.

Success Goal = 10 shadow swings

Your Score = (#) _____ shadow swings

2. Toss and Smash Drill

Stand near the net and toss a ball forward and high into the air. Get your racket back early, reach high, and smash the toss. Keep the ball in front of your body position and do not let it drop too low. Try to make the ball bounce high into the opposite court so that an opponent would not be able to make a return.

Success Goal = 8 out of 10 attempts into the opposite singles court

Your Score = (#) _____ smashes

3. Smash and Touch Drill

Start at the net, move back, and swing through the smash motion without hitting the ball, then move forward to touch the net. Remember to move back with your side (opposite shoulder) to the net.

Success Goal = 10 smash-and-touch combinations

Your Score = (#) _____ smash-and-touch combinations

4. Lob–Smash Combination Drill

Have a partner hit lobs from the baseline to you at the net. Return lobs with smashes as many times as possible. Start from the ready position, then turn early and take lots of small steps. Don't dig in too early.

Variation: Play the point out after the smash and keep score.

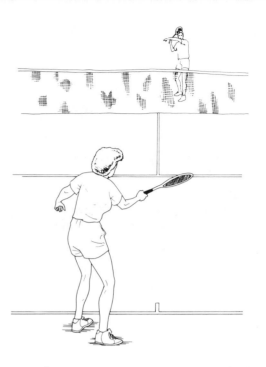

Success Goal = 10 smashes placed into the singles court

Your Score = (#) _____ smashes

5. Smash to Target Drill

Your partner hits lobs from the baseline to you at the net. Return lobs with smashes directed at large boxes or similar targets placed in these positions: deep backhand corner, deep forehand corner, just inside the singles sideline on the right-side service line, and at a similar location on the left-side service line. Position your feet so that they are aligned with the target you are trying to hit.

Variation: Compete against yourself or against a partner and keep score. If there are three of you, have two hit lobs and the other hit smashes before rotating.

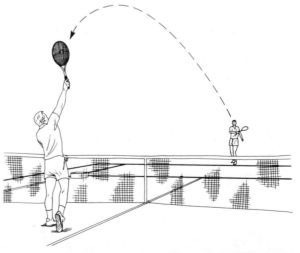

Success Goal = 4 out of 10 smashes to target

Your Score = (#) _____ target hits

6. One-on-One Lob Smash Drill

One player stands behind the baseline, and another puts the ball into play with a lob to the player at the net. Play the point out, using lobs and smashes.

Lobs and smashes go together; it's hard to practice one without practicing the other. When it's your turn to play the point out with a smash, do the best you can until you get more instruction. If you simply can't hit a smash, keep the ball in play with the best shot you can hit. Change positions after every 5-point game.

Success Goal = win at least half of the games played

Your Score = (#) _____ wins, (#) _____ losses

7. Smash–Lob Games

Take a position at the net; have a partner stand at the baseline, setting you up with lobs. Smash the lobs and play the points out. The first player to win 10 points wins the game. Change positions and repeat the drill.

Smash wide to open up the court. Don't smash to the same spot on consecutive shots unless your opponent moves to anticipate the next shot and you hit behind him or her.

Success Goal = win the game when hitting smashes

Your Score = (#) _____ games won when hitting smashes

Smash
Keys to Success to Checklist

The teacher or observer is going to watch your feet first on this shot, so make sure you move them quickly into place with lots of short steps. Get the racket back behind your head early (no full swing), turn your side to the net, keep the ball out in front of your body, and swing up (not forward) to hit. Timing can be difficult on smashes, so let the ball bounce if you can do that without giving up your offensive, attacking position on the court. Ask the observer to check your technique using this list.

Preparation Phase

_____ Smasher takes many small steps to get into position to hit a smash, not digging in too early, but moving feet as though playing defense in basketball.

_____ Player steps forward with the opposite foot before swinging, getting set to hit just as baseball players get set to throw.

_____ Smasher takes an abbreviated backswing by drawing the racket straight behind head before the shot, not taking a full windup. This will provide plenty of power with less chance of things going wrong.

_____ Player uses the Continental grip. The forehand grip will make too many shots sail out, and the backhand grip will make it hard to hit flat—put-away shots.

_____ Smasher keeps the ball out in front of body. Some players point to the ball with the opposite hand, then try to make contact at the spot where they are pointing.

Execution Phase

_____ Arm fully extends while reaching up to hit. Body is a straight arrow leaning forward during hit.

_____ Smasher hits the ball flat (without spin) when close to the net. At contact, the thumb moves forward, down, and across at the moment of contact (in other words, the wrist pronates).

Follow-Through
Phase

_____ The swing continues after contact with the ball. If there is a stop at contact, the shot will lack power and depth.

_____ The racket moves away from body, then down and across the front of body to finish the stroke. Out, down, and across—in that order.

_____ Smasher recovers to the ready position for the next shot. If the first smash does not finish the point, a second smash or forcing volley should do it.

Step 11 Volley-Lob-Smash Combinations

Now that you know what to do with the ball when you get to the net, several things can happen. If you are at the net, your opponent can hit either a groundstroke or a lob. If it is a groundstroke and you can get to it, make a return with a volley. If the other player lobs, then you have a chance to use your overhead smash. If you are both at the net, the one who hits the best volleys will win the point.

When you are at the baseline and your opponent is at the net, you have two choices: Try to win with groundstrokes that pass the net player or force an error, or lob over his or her head.

Whatever the situation, some combination of those three shots determine the outcome of the point. Following are some drills to help you practice this series of shots.

Volley-Lob-Smash Combination Drills

1. Up and Back Drill

Have a partner stand at the baseline with a basket of balls. You start at the net and move back to smash a lob fed to you by your partner. As soon as you hit the smash, move forward to volley a short drive set up by your partner with another ball. Continue for 20 sequences—10 smashes and 10 volleys.

Success Goal = 10 out of 20 shots in the singles court

Your Score = (#) _____ smashes and volleys

2. Lob-Smash Game

Start at the baseline and hit a lob to your partner at the net. Play the point out, using only lobs and smashes. First player to win 10 points wins. Then change positions.

Success Goal = win at least half the games played

Your Score = (#) _____ wins, (#) _____ losses

3. *Volley-Volley-Smash Drill*

Start at the net against a partner at the baseline with a basket of balls. Your partner sets you up for a forehand volley, then a backhand volley, then back for a smash. Use one ball, but have extra ones ready in case a ball goes out-of-play. Repeat the cycle 5 times (15 shots), then change positions.

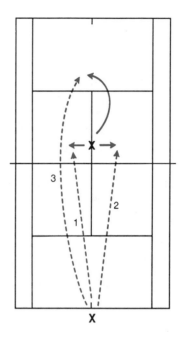

Success Goal = 10 out of 15 attempts

Your Score = (#) _____ returns

4. *Volley-Lob Drill*

Start at the net with your partner at the baseline. Your partner puts the ball in play by dropping and hitting a forehand drive to you at the net. Return the drive with a volley deep to the backcourt. Your partner then lobs, trying to make the ball land in your backcourt. Do not try to return the lob. You get 1 point if your volley goes into the backcourt. Your partner gets 1 point if his or her lob hits in your backcourt. Change positions after 10 points.

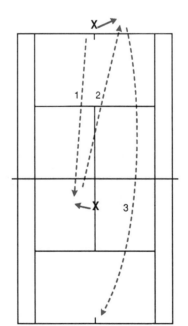

Success Goal =

   a. 5 out of 10 volleys into the backcourt

   b. 5 out of 10 lobs into the backcourt

Your Score =

   a. (#) _____ volleys hit into backcourt

   b. (#) _____ lobs hit into backcourt

5. High-Low Drill

Take a position at the net and have a practice partner hit 5 two-shot sequences. Each first shot should be set up for you to return with a high backhand (like a low lob that you can barely reach by turning and stretching with your racket extended). The second shot should be low and to your forehand side.

Hit a total of 10 shots—5 high backhand volleys and 5 low forehand volleys. Then change the sequence to hit high forehand and low backhand volleys.

Success Goal =

a. 6 of 10 high backhands, low forehands

b. 6 of 10 high forehands, low backhands

Your Score =

a. (#) _____ returns using sequence a

b. (#) _____ returns using sequence b

Step 12   Advanced Volley

At this level of the game, the volley becomes more than just a shot hit before the ball bounces on your side of the court. Now it should be an important part of your offensive and defensive game plan. There are a few fundamentals to master, but the position on the court from which you hit volleys and the playing levels of your opponents require good technique, pace, and location. It should be a quick and solid stroke that tells your opponent and anyone watching that they are dealing with someone who can play the entire court.

WHY IS THE ADVANCED VOLLEY IMPORTANT?

This stroke allows you to play from any position on the court with confidence and with the possibility of winning every point. Without a forceful volley, you would have to stay on the baseline and hit groundstroke after groundstroke, hoping your opponent would make an error. With the advanced volley, you can move to the forecourt area, force the action, and put shots away with authority.

The volley is even more important in doubles, where most of the points are won and lost at the net. In both singles and doubles, though, a good volley can help you improve your position on the court and move

in for a winner. As a defensive stroke, it can keep you out of trouble and in the point until you get an opportunity to go on the attack again.

HOW TO EXECUTE THE ADVANCED VOLLEY

The main difference between this shot and the beginner's volley is that here most intermediate and advanced players use the Continental grip. Remember that a Continental grip is the one in which you position your wrist directly above the top part of the racket handle (look at Figures 3.3a and b in Step 3). You hit all shots with the same grip—no changing from forehand to backhand. The reason you cannot effectively change grips is because you do not have time to change when you are at the net against good players.

Everything else about the shot is the same as with the beginner's volley. Imagine that a rope is tied between the net and the top of your racket frame, allowing you to draw the racket back just enough to punch through the ball forcefully. Now you will use the volley more frequently and with less preparation because at this level you are more often in a position near the net to use it (see Figure 12.1).

Figure 12.1 Keys to Success:
  Advanced Volley

**Preparation
Phase**

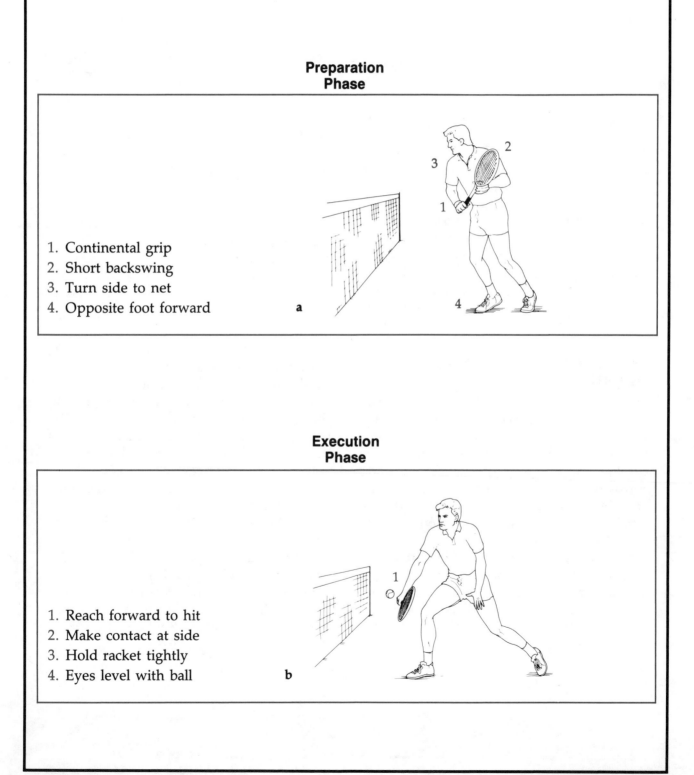

1. Continental grip
2. Short backswing
3. Turn side to net
4. Opposite foot forward

a

**Execution
Phase**

1. Reach forward to hit
2. Make contact at side
3. Hold racket tightly
4. Eyes level with ball

b

**Follow-Through
Phase**

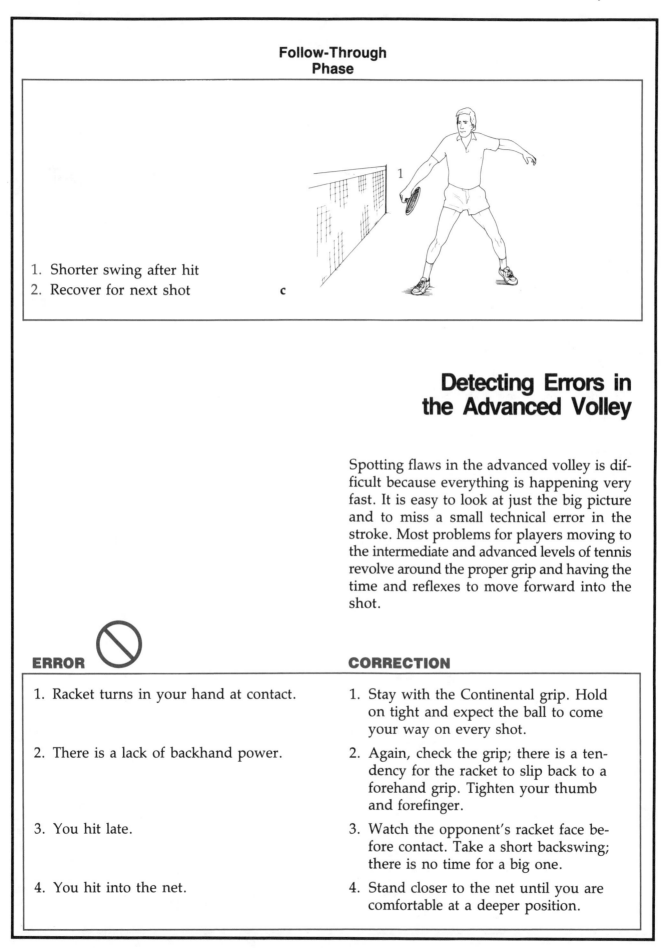

1. Shorter swing after hit
2. Recover for next shot

c

Detecting Errors in the Advanced Volley

Spotting flaws in the advanced volley is difficult because everything is happening very fast. It is easy to look at just the big picture and to miss a small technical error in the stroke. Most problems for players moving to the intermediate and advanced levels of tennis revolve around the proper grip and having the time and reflexes to move forward into the shot.

ERROR

CORRECTION

1. Racket turns in your hand at contact.	1. Stay with the Continental grip. Hold on tight and expect the ball to come your way on every shot.
2. There is a lack of backhand power.	2. Again, check the grip; there is a tendency for the racket to slip back to a forehand grip. Tighten your thumb and forefinger.
3. You hit late.	3. Watch the opponent's racket face before contact. Take a short backswing; there is no time for a big one.
4. You hit into the net.	4. Stand closer to the net until you are comfortable at a deeper position.

Advanced Volley Drills

1. Two-on-One Volley Drill

Volley against two partners, who alternate hitting shots to you at the net. If the shot comes low, get down low by bending your knees, and bump the ball deep and down the middle of the backcourt. If the ball comes at least shoulder high, volley at an angle to open the court. Score 1 point for every successful volley hit into the opposite singles court.

Variation: Place volleys into target areas, such as the right or left backcourt.

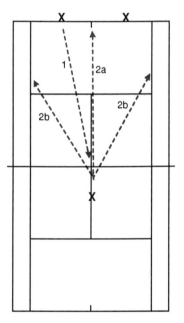

Success Goal = 15 out of 20 volleys hit into the target zone

Your Score = (#) _____ volleys

2. Target Volley Drill

Place a large cardboard box on the court. Start with the target in the deep backhand corner, then move it to the deep forehand corner, then short and wide to the backhand, and finally short and wide to the forehand side. Your partner drops and hits to set you up with shots to volley at the target.

Variation: Alternately hit forehand and backhand volleys without changing grips. Now move the target to different areas on the court.

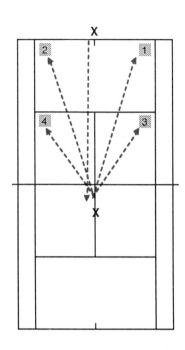

Success Goal = hit each target 5 out of 10 times

Your Score =

    a. (#) _____ target hits to the deep backhand corner (1)

    b. (#) _____ target hits to the deep forehand corner (2)

    c. (#) _____ target hits short and wide to the backhand side (3)

    d. (#) _____ target hits short and wide to the forehand side (4)

3. Consecutive Partner Volley Drill

You and your partner stand about 15 feet from the net, and on opposite sides of the net. Count the number of consecutive shots you hit to each other using only volleys.

  Begin the drill hitting soft, controlled volleys. Gradually pick up the pace as long as you can control the ball.

Variation: Stand in crosscourt positions and use only forehand or backhand volleys, depending on the side where you are positioned.

Success Goal = 15 consecutive volleys between you and your partner.

Your Score = (#) _____ volleys

4. Defend Your Turf Drill

Stand in one service court near the net and defend this area with volleys against shots put into play by your practice partner. Successful volleys go into the service court area.

Success Goal = return 15 out of 20 shots

Your Score = (#) _____ volley returns

5. Volley-Volley Up Drill

Stand at the service line opposite your partner, who is at the other service line. Keep the ball in play hitting consecutive volleys. With each volley, though, bump the ball up into the air to yourself, then hit it across the net to your partner, who does the same thing.

This drill helps you develop touch and take speed off the ball. There are times when touch and change of pace are just as effective as power.

Success Goal = 6 consecutive exchanges

Your Score = (#) _____ exchanges

6. Three at the Net Drill

Take a position just inside the service line against two players standing in the opposite service courts, each near one of the singles sidelines. Keep the ball in play, volleys alternating between the players across the net. Change positions every 3 minutes.

Success Goal = 9 consecutive volleys

Your Score = (#) _____ volleys

7. Closing Volley Drill

Start at the service line against a partner at the opposite service line. After putting the ball into play, hit consecutive volleys, each of you moving one step closer after each shot until you are at point-blank range at the net. With each error, begin at the service line again.

Success Goal = 2 series of volleys in which both partners are within two steps of the net without a miss

Your Score = (#) _____ series of volleys

8. Change-of-Pace Volley Drill

Take a volleying position at the net, with a partner at the opposite baseline. Have your partner feed you shots. Return the shots, alternately with forcing volleys and softer, controlled volleys.

Hit forceful volleys by moving the racket head quickly through the path of the ball and following through completely. Take pace off of the ball by taking a shorter backswing, reducing the speed of the racket, and shortening the follow-through. Change positions every 3 minutes.

Success Goal = 8 consecutive ''in'' volleys, alternating between hard-hit and soft-hit shots

Your Score = (#) _____ volleys

9. Hand-Behind-the-Back Volley Drill

Take a volleying position at the net, with a partner at the opposite baseline. Hold your racket with a Continental grip; put your other hand behind your back. Keep the ball in play using the Continental grip; keep your other hand out of the way (to avoid the temptation of changing grips, and to build strength in the forearm).

Success Goal = 3 minutes of hitting without changing grips or using the other hand to help

Your Score = (#) _____ minutes

10. *Wall Volley Drill*

Stand 15 feet from a rebound net or wall and keep the ball in play against the wall, hitting volleys only. This is a difficult drill. Start out hitting with just enough force to make the ball come back to you. Recover quickly after each hit. There won't be time to change grips.

Variation: Alternately hit forehand and backhand volleys.

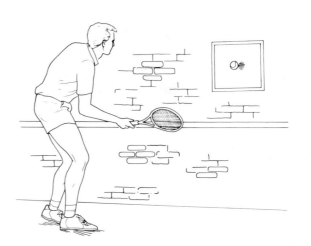

Success Goal = 12 consecutive volleys

Your Score = (#) _____ volleys

11. *Lunge Volley Drill*

Take a volleying position at the net against a partner at the opposite baseline. Have your partner hit drives as wide as possible (without going out-of-bounds) to your backhand side. Holding a Continental grip, quickly lunge to that side—turning your back, if necessary, in order to reach farther—to get the ball back. Recover quickly for the next shot.

Success Goal = 5 consecutive lunge volleys back into the singles court

Your Score = (#) _____ volleys

12. *Volley-Lob-Retrieve Drill*

You and a practice partner take positions just inside opposite service lines in the middle of the court. Exchange at least 5 volleys, then the partner previously agreed-upon hits a lob volley over the other's head. That player retreats, returns the lob after the bounce, then works his or her way back to the service line to continue the series of volleys. After 5 more consecutive volleys, the second partner (the one who had retrieved the lob) hits a lob volley. Consider this entire sequence a *round*.

This is a very difficult drill and requires at least intermediate and possibly advanced skills. At this point, you may practice this drill or move on to Drill 13 or Drill 14.

Success Goal = 2 rounds of volleys followed by lobs

Your Score = (#) _____ rounds

13. Crosscourt Volley Drill

Take a position inside the service line and slightly to either side of the center service line. Have a partner give setup shots that go down the line to your forehand side. Return the setups with crosscourt volleys. Remember to move forward as you move to the side for the volley.

Hit 20 crosscourt volleys on your forehand side, then have your partner set up shots for you to return crosscourt with backhand volleys.

Success Goal =

   a. 15 out of 20 forehand crosscourt volleys

   b. 15 out of 20 backhand crosscourt volleys

Your Score =

   a. (#) _____ forehand crosscourt volleys

   b. (#) _____ backhand crosscourt volleys

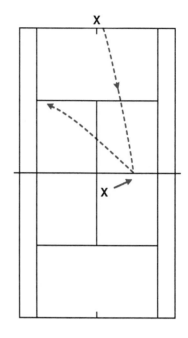

14. Down-the-Line Volley Drill

Take a position in the center of the court inside the service line. Have your partner stand slightly to one side of the center mark on the baseline and set you up with crosscourt groundstrokes. Return the crosscourt shots with volleys hit down-the-line, parallel to the line closest to you. Hit 20 down-the-line volleys with your forehand and 20 with your backhand.

Success Goal =

   a. 15 out of 20 forehand down-the-line volleys

   b. 15 out of 20 backhand down-the-line volleys

Your Score =

   a. (#) _____ forehand down-the-line volleys

   b. (#) _____ backhand down-the-line volleys

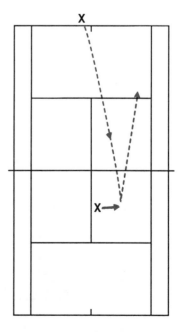

Advanced Volley
Keys to Success Checklist

The first thing a teacher will watch for in the advanced volley is your grip. Make sure you know the difference between a Continental grip and those you have learned for the forehand and backhand. Take a short backswing, step forward, and hold your racket tightly for solid contact. Don't wait for the ball to come to you—go get it early. Anybody can look good on the forehand volley, but only advanced players can execute the backhand volley in a way that is comfortable, accurate, and powerful. Ask your teacher or another trained observer to check your technique using this checklist.

**Preparation
Phase**

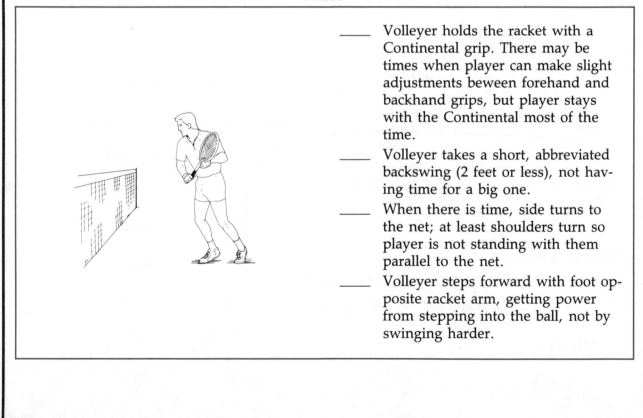

_____ Volleyer holds the racket with a Continental grip. There may be times when player can make slight adjustments beween forehand and backhand grips, but player stays with the Continental most of the time.

_____ Volleyer takes a short, abbreviated backswing (2 feet or less), not having time for a big one.

_____ When there is time, side turns to the net; at least shoulders turn so player is not standing with them parallel to the net.

_____ Volleyer steps forward with foot opposite racket arm, getting power from stepping into the ball, not by swinging harder.

Execution
Phase

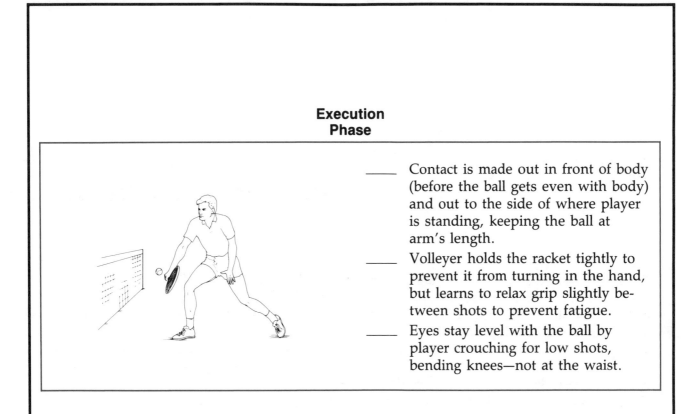

_____ Contact is made out in front of body (before the ball gets even with body) and out to the side of where player is standing, keeping the ball at arm's length.

_____ Volleyer holds the racket tightly to prevent it from turning in the hand, but learns to relax grip slightly between shots to prevent fatigue.

_____ Eyes stay level with the ball by player crouching for low shots, bending knees—not at the waist.

Follow-Through
Phase

_____ The swing finishes with a shorter, quicker motion than with groundstrokes. On forceful volleys, there may be times when swing can finish with a more complete follow-through, but most of the time player should punch through the shot with a shorter motion from preparation to follow-through.

_____ Volleyer recovers quickly for the next shot, getting the racket right back up in front of body (with the racket head high) in anticipation of the next shot.

Step 13   **Half Volley**

The *half volley* is a shot hit immediately after the ball has hit the court. Baseball players catch balls on the "short hop," right after it bounces in front of them. Tennis players have to field a half volley similarly, but they do it with a racket. The shot is actually a forehand or backhand groundstroke, but the fundamentals are similar to a volley, so it is called a *half volley*—half volley, half groundstroke.

WHY IS THE HALF VOLLEY IMPORTANT?

This is a shot you don't want to hit unless you have to. It usually means that you are out of position, you have prepared late, or your opponent has hit a forcing shot. In any case, the ball comes hard at your feet, and you have to dig it out and get it back. It is emergency tennis at its best—or worst. Unfortunately, the older you get, the slower your reaction time, and the more you find yourself out of position. So start working on your court position, but also be ready to return those forcing shots, when necessary.

HOW TO EXECUTE THE HALF VOLLEY

Because there is little time to react, there are few things to remember about the half volley. Turn your side or at least your shoulders as soon as you know on which side you will have to take the ball. If you can turn early, you can draw back your racket early.

There is no time to take a big backswing, so severely restrict that part of the hitting motion. Also, if you take a big backswing, there is a tendency to overhit the ball. All you need to do is block this shot; big swings are not only time-consuming—they are counterproductive.

After you have turned your side to the net, crouch (as though you were sitting on a stool or bench) while you hit. Try to see the ball at eye level and stay down low throughout the shot. As you swing forward, block the ball and try to make contact out in front of your position. Lift the racket head as you make contact, in order to get the ball over the net.

On balls that come at you without a lot of pace, the follow-through is relatively normal. Hit through the ball and continue your swing. On hard-hit shots, just block the ball as it leaves the court surface and don't worry about a follow-through. Aim your strings in the right direction, hold tight, and watch what happens (see Figure 13.1).

Figure 13.1 Keys to Success: Half Volley

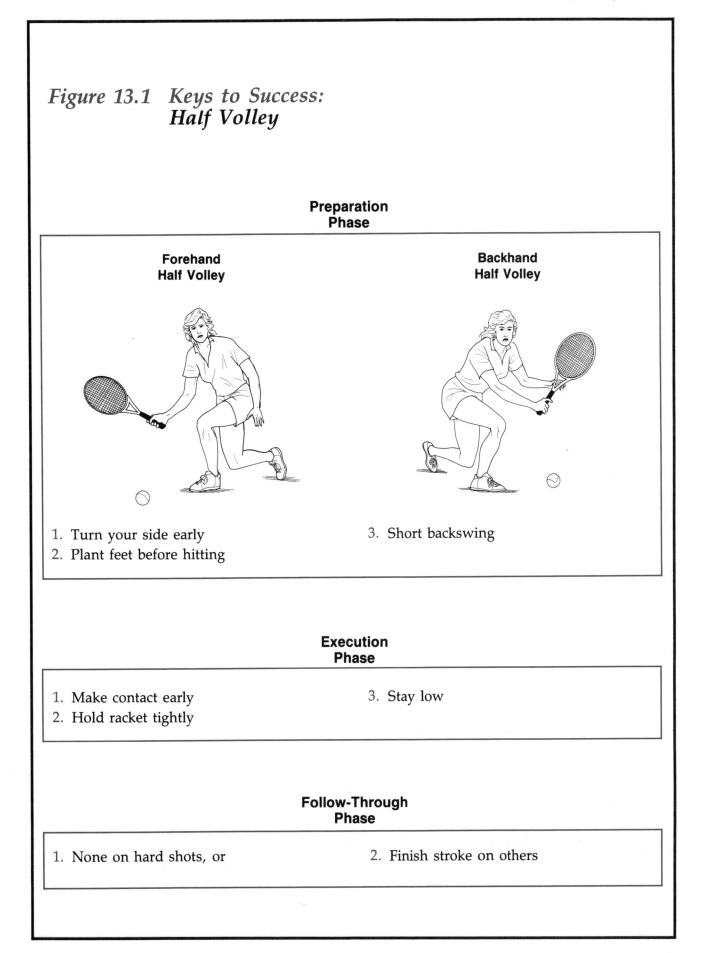

Preparation Phase

Forehand Half Volley

Backhand Half Volley

1. Turn your side early
2. Plant feet before hitting

3. Short backswing

Execution Phase

1. Make contact early
2. Hold racket tightly

3. Stay low

Follow-Through Phase

1. None on hard shots, or

2. Finish stroke on others

Detecting Errors in the Half Volley

It takes a trained eye to spot problems with this stroke because everything happens very fast. Have someone help you watch for these problems.

ERROR 🚫

CORRECTION

ERROR	CORRECTION
1. Racket turns in hand on contact.	1. Hold on tighter.
2. You hit too deep.	2. Just block the ball—do not swing at it or try to fight power with power.
3. You hit late and to the side.	3. Shorten your backswing; there isn't enough time for a full one.
4. You have to hit too many half volleys.	4. Stay out of the no-man's-land between the baseline and the service line.

Half Volley Drills

1. Quick Hit Drill

Stand in the middle of the court one step behind the service line. Drop and hit 20 shots on your forehand side, trying to make contact as quickly after the ball bounces as possible. Listen for the "bang-bang" sound of the ball hitting the court, then being hit by your racket strings.

Success Goal = 15 of 20 attempts hit into the opposite singles court

Your Score = (#) _____ half volleys

2. No-Man's-Land Rally Drill

Take a position between the baseline and the service line. Keep the ball in play against a partner at the baseline with controlled shots, including those hit with the short-hop half volley. Although this is not a good position for match play, it forces you to practice shots that may help your game later.

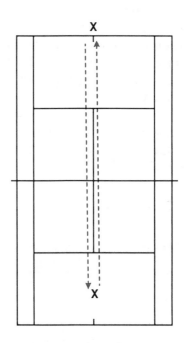

Success Goal = return 4 of 5 attempted half volleys

Your Score = (#) _____ returns

3. Close-In Service Return Drill

Have a partner practice the serve while you practice returns from a position one step behind the service line. Turn your shoulders quickly and take a restricted backswing. This drill not only helps your half volley, but it also improves your return of serve and your quickness.

Success Goal = return 3 out of 10 attempts

Your Score = (#) _____ returns

4. Hot Seat Half-Volley Drill

One player stands at the baseline with a basket of balls. Two players stand at the net opposite you. You stand on the service line on the side with the baseline player. That player sets up the volleyers, who hit shots directly at you. Dig out as many shots as you can with volleys and half volleys.

Be especially aggressive when you are volleying against the other two players. The odds are against you. Don't be nice.

Success Goal = return 2 out of 10 attempts

Your Score = (#) _____ returns

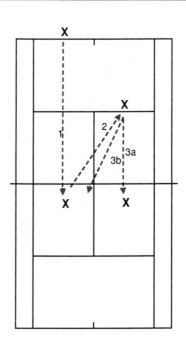

5. Baseline Half-Volley Drill

Your partner stands at the net with a basket of balls and drives balls hard at your feet on the baseline. Quick hands are the key to surviving this drill. Forget technique and fight to keep the ball in play.

Success Goal = 4 out of 10 attempts

Your Score = (#) _____ attempts

Half Volley
Keys to Success Checklist

The observer should watch for things like a quick shoulder turn, a short backswing, and a low body position. But what he or she is really going to notice is whether you can return hard-hit balls with a half volley. More than with any other stroke, the test is whether the ball goes back over the net. Keep your eyes wide open, hold your racket tightly, and get it low enough to dig the ball out of the court. This shot will test your reflexes and your will more than your technique. Nevertheless, ask a trained observer to use this checklist.

Preparation Phase

Forehand Half Volley

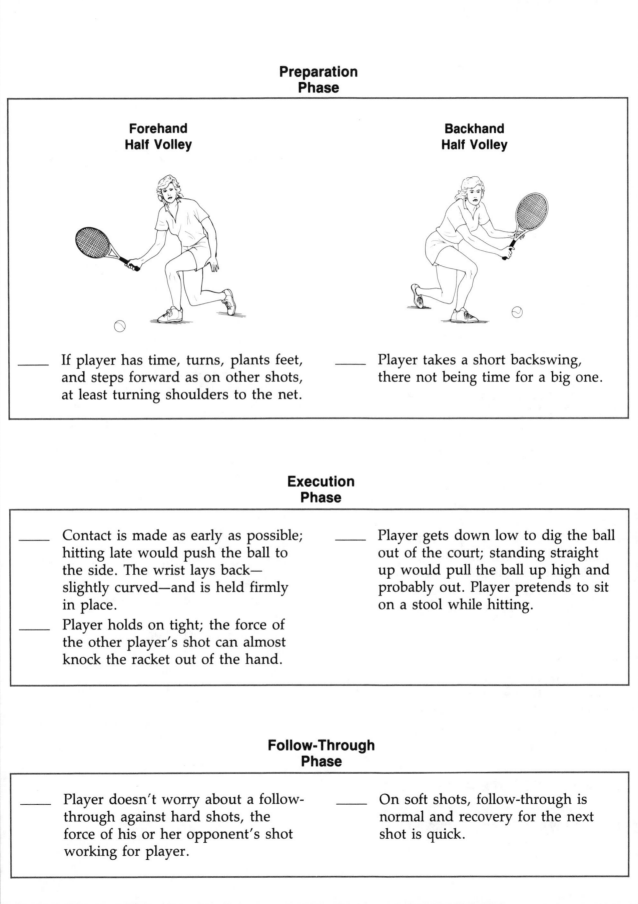

Backhand Half Volley

_____ If player has time, turns, plants feet, and steps forward as on other shots, at least turning shoulders to the net.

_____ Player takes a short backswing, there not being time for a big one.

Execution Phase

_____ Contact is made as early as possible; hitting late would push the ball to the side. The wrist lays back—slightly curved—and is held firmly in place.

_____ Player holds on tight; the force of the other player's shot can almost knock the racket out of the hand.

_____ Player gets down low to dig the ball out of the court; standing straight up would pull the ball up high and probably out. Player pretends to sit on a stool while hitting.

Follow-Through Phase

_____ Player doesn't worry about a follow-through against hard shots, the force of his or her opponent's shot working for player.

_____ On soft shots, follow-through is normal and recovery for the next shot is quick.

Step 14   Drop Shot

A *drop shot* floats softly into the opponent's forecourt area and bounces twice before the other player can get to it. This kind of shot usually follows a series of strokes and comes when the opponent expects something hard and deep. Although it can be used by any player, a well-hit drop shot is a relatively sophisticated shot used by intermediate and advanced players.

WHY IS THE DROP SHOT IMPORTANT?

This shot is effective against players who are out of position, out of shape, or who do not cover the court well. It also works well against opponents who are tired, lazy, or both. If you use the shot often enough, your opponent's concern that you might use it again can make other shots from a similar position on the court become more effective.

For example, if the other player hits a weak shot that bounces inside your service court, you could move in to crunch it deep into the other backcourt. Knowing this, your opponent will probably start preparing to defend that kind of shot. You set up to hit the anticipated shot, but instead execute a delicate drop that barely clears the net. Just like the other strokes and their variations, this shot gives you one more option and gives your opponents one more problem.

HOW TO EXECUTE A DROP SHOT

The drop shot preparation should look like that for any other shot you might hit from the forecourt. This is *disguising* the shot, which means no exaggerated backswing, no delay in the stroke, no change in footwork, and no difference in facial expression. Hold the racket firmly but not overly tight, open the racket face slightly, and delicately slide the racket face under the ball as you make contact. Start the racket head above the level of your waist and swing down on the ball. The high-to-low swing and the open racket face should give the shot a bit of backspin. Shots played after the bounce require an abbreviated follow-through. *Drop volleys* (drop shots hit with volleys) are also more effective if the follow-through is abbreviated.

Hit the drop shot so that the ball falls in a downward direction as it clears the net. Barely clearing the net is effective, but not absolutely necessary. The thing to avoid is hitting the ball so that it travels too far toward your opponent after the bounce. Putting backspin on the ball by hitting with an open racket face should make it bite into the court and slow down (see Figure 14.1).

Expect the other player to reach the ball and return it. If it is not returned, you win the point; if it is, you should be near the net and ready to volley the ball for a winner. Hitting drop shots on consecutive points may be a good idea if the other player has to work hard to get to the ball on the first drop shot.

Figure 14.1 **Keys to Success:**
Drop Shot

Preparation Phase

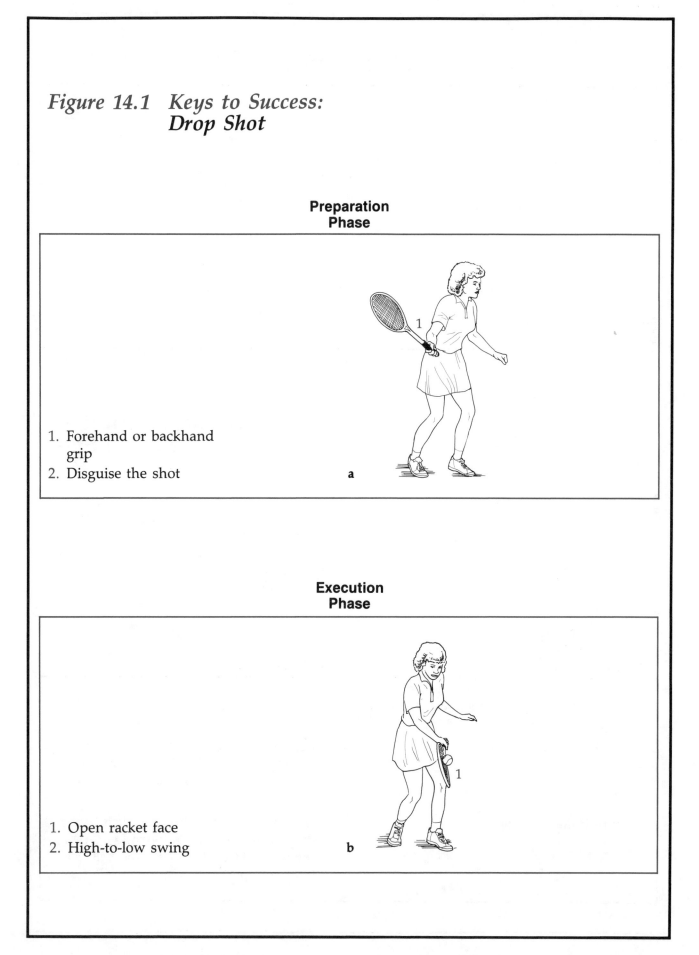

1. Forehand or backhand grip
2. Disguise the shot

a

Execution Phase

1. Open racket face
2. High-to-low swing

b

**Follow-Through
Phase**

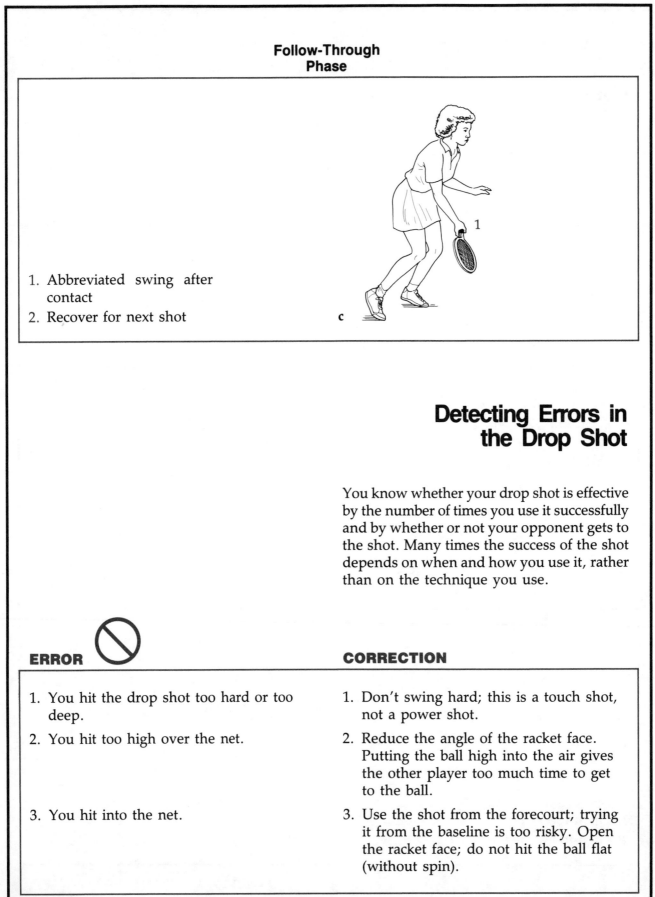

1. Abbreviated swing after contact
2. Recover for next shot

c

Detecting Errors in the Drop Shot

You know whether your drop shot is effective by the number of times you use it successfully and by whether or not your opponent gets to the shot. Many times the success of the shot depends on when and how you use it, rather than on the technique you use.

ERROR	CORRECTION
1. You hit the drop shot too hard or too deep.	1. Don't swing hard; this is a touch shot, not a power shot.
2. You hit too high over the net.	2. Reduce the angle of the racket face. Putting the ball high into the air gives the other player too much time to get to the ball.
3. You hit into the net.	3. Use the shot from the forecourt; trying it from the baseline is too risky. Open the racket face; do not hit the ball flat (without spin).

Drop Shot Drills

1. Drop-and-Hit Drop Shot Drills

Stand at the service line, drop the ball, and hit into the opposite service court. Use your forehand to practice this drill; make it look as much like your normal forehand swing as possible.

Variation: Make the ball bounce at least twice before it crosses the opponent's service line.

Success Goal = 8 out of 10 attempts into the service court

Your Score = (#) _____ attempts

2. Drop Shot Setup Drill

Stand in the center of the court just behind the service line. Have your partner, on the other side, drop and hit shots that bounce between you and the net. Return each setup with a drop shot. Relax your grip slightly in order to have a better "feel" for the shot.

Variation: Compete by counting 1 point for every shot your partner places inside your service court for a setup, and 1 point for each you return as a successful drop shot.

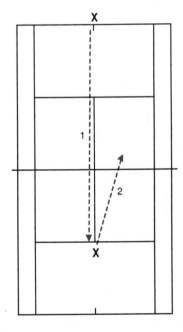

Success Goal = 5 out of 10 attempts returned to the service court

Your Score = (#) _____ drop shots

3. Drop Shot Point Drill

Stand just behind your service line and have an opponent stand at the opposite baseline. Your opponent drops and hits 10 shots into the forecourt. You return with a drop shot and play the point out.

Disguise your shot. Try to anticipate what your opponent will do if he or she gets to your drop shot.

Variation: Change the rules to allow the player at the net to hit any shot. With this variation, you will not know whether to charge forward after the setup.

Success Goal = win at least half the points played

Your Score = (#) _____ points won out of (#) _____ points played

4. Short Game

Play a game against your partner, using only drop shots. Any ball hit hard or that bounces outside of the service court area is out-of-play. Put the ball into play with a soft drop-and-hit forehand.

Variation: One player hits all down-the-line drop shots, and the other hits all crosscourt drop shots.

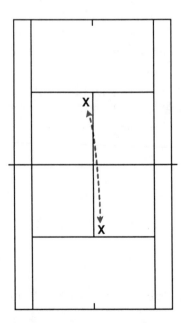

Success Goal = win at least half the games played

Your Score = (#) _____ wins, (#) _____ losses

Drop Shot
Keys to Success Checklist

The keys to making the drop shot effective are to make it look like any other shot until just before contact and to make the ball "die" in the opponent's forecourt. Use either a forehand or backhand grip, depending on which side the ball is hit, open the racket face, swing from high to low, and use a delicate touch when the strings hit the ball. To make the drop shot safer, use as much of the opposite service court as needed by hitting at an angle (rather than hitting straight ahead).

**Preparation
Phase**

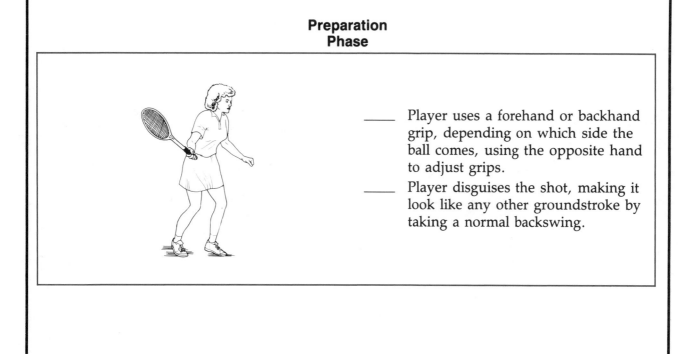

_____ Player uses a forehand or backhand grip, depending on which side the ball comes, using the opposite hand to adjust grips.

_____ Player disguises the shot, making it look like any other groundstroke by taking a normal backswing.

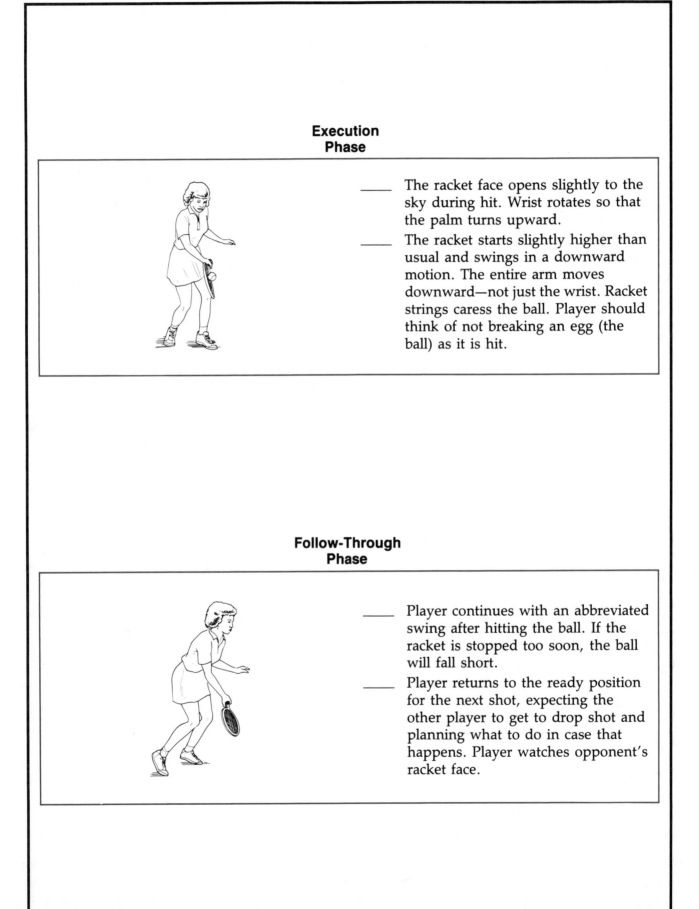

Execution Phase

_____ The racket face opens slightly to the sky during hit. Wrist rotates so that the palm turns upward.

_____ The racket starts slightly higher than usual and swings in a downward motion. The entire arm moves downward—not just the wrist. Racket strings caress the ball. Player should think of not breaking an egg (the ball) as it is hit.

Follow-Through Phase

_____ Player continues with an abbreviated swing after hitting the ball. If the racket is stopped too soon, the ball will fall short.

_____ Player returns to the ready position for the next shot, expecting the other player to get to drop shot and planning what to do in case that happens. Player watches opponent's racket face.

Step 15   Using Your Strokes in Singles

You can decide on the style of singles play best for you. Some players are more comfortable at the baseline and are very successful at developing a strong game based on the strokes used in that part of the court. They depend on preparation, consistency, patience, and endurance to defeat opponents. Others would rather advance to the net as much as possible and try to win with strong serves, volleys, and smashes. Power, speed, and quickness are essential for such a style of play. A third group can play effectively from any position on the court. They vary their styles depending on the opponents, the kind of court, and the strokes that are working well for them at the time.

HOW TO USE GROUNDSTROKES

Good forehands and backhands can keep you in the point, make opponents move and leave part of the court open, give them chances to make errors, set you up for winners, and allow you to apply constant pressure. In singles, groundstrokes are the basic tools to help you put together a winning game plan. Use the following suggestions to help you improve your groundstrokes. It is important that you focus on only one suggestion at a time.

- *Move to a position behind the center of the baseline between groundstrokes* (Diagram 15.1). As soon as you hit a shot, start moving back to your base of operations; do not wait to see where the ball is going. As the point develops, you move from that central baseline position. When in doubt, though, go to that spot.

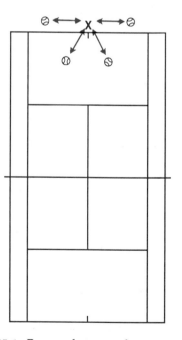

Diagram 15.1   Recover between shots.

- *Hit most baseline groundstrokes crosscourt.* There is more distance to work with from corner to corner, and the net is lower in the middle than it is on the sides.
- *Hit most baseline groundstrokes deep into the court.* Deep shots keep your opponent from attacking.
- *From the forecourt, hit shots at an angle to open up the court* (Diagram 15.2). Hitting angled shots forces your opponent to run wide for returns; this gives you open space to hit winners.
- *Use a shorter backswing against power players.* There is not enough time to take big windups.
- *Use a shorter backswing on an approach shot (shot you hit right before you move in toward the net).* Because you are already moving forward, your body provides plenty of power without your taking a full backswing.
- *Use a shorter backswing against fast serves.* Again, there is not enough time for anything else.
- *Keep the ball low when trying to pass an opponent at the net.* If you put the shot up too high, the player at the net would have time to get to the ball and hit down on it for a winning volley.
- *During a baseline rally, develop a pattern, then break it* (Diagram 15.3). The combination of patterns is almost endless, but the idea is to lull your opponent into a supposedly predictable series of exchanges, then change the pattern when it is least expected.
- *If you are weak on one side, tempt the other player to hit to your strong side by leaving part of the court open.* If you know the shot will be returned into a specific part of the court, you can prepare early to hit it.

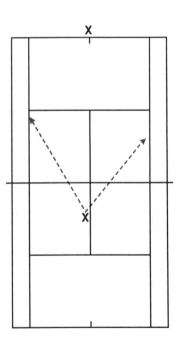

Diagram 15.2 Open the court with angled shots.

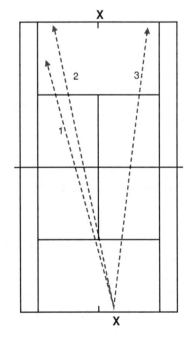

Diagram 15.3 Break a groundstroke pattern.

- *Stand near the baseline in the middle of the two extreme sides to which the ball can be served* (Diagram 15.4). Every server is limited in how wide he or she can serve the ball by service court lines, by the serving position on the baseline, and by laws of physics. Stand at a point where you can cover the widest possible angles of the serve.
- *Return short, weak serves down the line closer to your position on the court* (Diagram 15.5). Put pressure on your opponent and open up the court for the next shot.

HOW TO USE THE SERVE

The first priority for the serve in singles is to get the ball into play. If you can do this without any problems, then you can begin to move the ball around the service court with varieties

of pace and spin. If you are not getting at least 70% of your first serves in, reduce the pace. Focus on only one of the following suggestions at a time:

- *Stand near the center of the baseline to serve* (see Diagram 15.4). From this point you are as close to every other part of the court as you can be while serving, and in the best possible starting position to make your next shot. Move away from the central position as long as you can cover the whole court after the serve.
- *Do not waste energy trying to serve aces (service winners).* Let your opponent know you are capable of hitting an ace now and then, but save trying the shot for times when you are comfortably ahead or when you have run especially hard during the previous point and don't want to get caught up in another long rally.

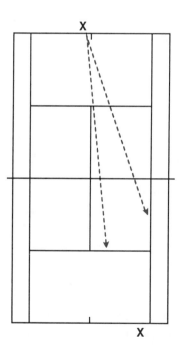

Diagram 15.4 Cover the widest possible angles.

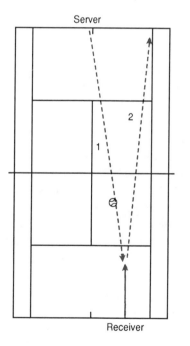

Diagram 15.5 Return down-the-line on short, weak serves.

- *Develop two medium-paced serves, rather than one fast serve and one slow one.* Accurately placed serves are just as effective and more consistent than power serves followed by very weak second serves.
- *Serve to an opponent's weakness or to an open area.* The weakest side is the backhand for most players, but you have to confirm this during the warm-up or as the match progresses. The open area depends on where your opponent lines up to receive. Many players try to protect their backhands by moving a step or two in the direction of their backhands. This leaves an open spot on the forehand side, which may be an appropriate target in some cases. Serve from the right side deep and down the middle when playing right-handers. From the left side, serve deep and to the outside of the service court.
- *Be careful about serving to the receiver's forehand.* Even though the other player may leave you some daylight, it is probably his or her strongest side. Experiment with the wide-to-the-right serve, but if it does not work, go back to a more conventional strategy.
- *Serve wide to pull an opponent off the court.* If you can do this, there will be more of the court open to the opposite side for your next shot.
- *Serve deep into the service court to keep your opponent from attacking you on the service return.* The more distance you can keep between your opponent and the net, the more difficult it becomes for that player to play aggressively.
- *Use spin on the serve for more control.* Remember: Hit the ball flat (without spin) for power and with a slice or topspin to make the ball curve down and into the court.
- *When serving, play more conservatively when the score is tied or when you are losing late in a game.* If the score is close, you still have a chance to win because the serve gives you an advantage. Do not choke and start punching at the ball, but be patient and selective about when to hit forcing shots and when to move in to the net.
- *Experiment with a variety of serves during a match.* The object is to keep your opponent guessing about how hard you will hit, where the ball is going, and how much spin the ball will have. Don't let a player get into a service return groove. If you play someone who just cannot handle a particular serve, use it most of the time, otherwise, move the ball around the service court.

HOW TO USE THE VOLLEY

Although it is possible to develop a strong baseline singles game, a complete player develops the ability to volley from positions all over the court. Look for openings to get into volleying positions. Force your opponent into positions in which part of the court is left open, then move in for the kill with well-placed volleys. Use the following suggestions to help you improve your volleys. Focus on only one suggestion at a time.

- *Stand near the center of the court 10–15 feet from the net to hit most volleys.* This position changes as the angle of your opponent's return changes. If that player is pulled off to the side of the court to make a return, you have to move in that direction to cover the angle from the new position. There are times when you have to play closer to the net or farther from it than 10–15 feet. If you are really attacking and get an easy shot to volley, you may be practically on top of the net before you hit. After a weak approach shot, you may be forced to play a volley on or behind the service line.
- *Place most volleys deep and into the open part of the court.* If you keep the ball deep, there is less chance of being passed when your volley does not win the point outright. Hitting to the "open part of the court" means placing the ball to a part of the court left unprotected by your opponent. Look for daylight when you are preparing to hit and block the ball in that direction.
- *Use a crosscourt volley to return a shot hit down-the-line* (Diagram 15.6). A down-the-

line attempt by your opponent gives you a good crosscourt angle for the next shot.

- *Use a down-the-line volley to return a shot hit crosscourt* (Diagram 15.7). The reverse of the previous situation is also true. If you are at the net and the ball goes crosscourt, a down-the-line volley should win the point because that is where the open space is.

- *When you move to one side to hit a volley, try to move slightly forward as you go to the ball* (Diagram 15.8). Because you are taking a short backswing on the shot, the only way to get power is to move diagonally toward the ball. Moving at a 45-degree angle into the shot allows you to use your body weight transfer to compensate for the lack of a bigger backswing.

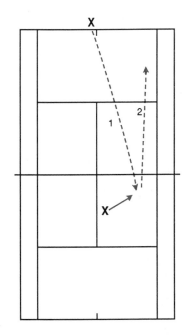

Diagram 15.7 Use a down-the-line volley against crosscourt passing shots.

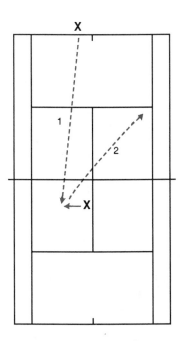

Diagram 15.6 Use a crosscourt volley against down-the-line passing shots.

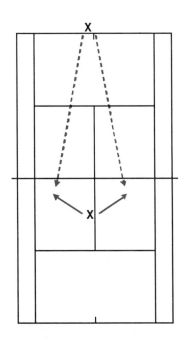

Diagram 15.8 Move forward to hit volleys.

- *Move closer to the net after a well-hit volley.* By "closing" after a good shot, you improve your court position and maintain your role as the attacker. If you volley and stay in the same place, you may be passed or have to hit up on the next shot.
- *Use the first volley to set yourself up for a winning second volley.* The first volley does not have to be a winner. If you can place the ball deep or at a good angle, you can go for the put-away on the second shot. Never attempt a difficult shot when a less difficult one can accomplish just as much. If you hit a good enough approach shot, a simple tap on the volley will probably set you up to win the point.
- *When in doubt, volley deep to your opponent's weakest side.* This at least gives you more time to decide what to do with the next shot—if you get one.
- *Expect every shot to come back to you following a volley.* The pace of the point is much quicker at the net. You do not have time to admire your shots as you do sometimes from the baseline. Hit the volley, close toward the net, and immediately get your racket out in front for the next shot.

HOW TO USE THE LOB

The lob is one of the most effective shots in singles, especially against very aggressive players and against those who have weak smashes. Use it at least often enough to keep your opponent off-balance. If it works, use it more regularly. Focus on only one of the following suggestions at a time:

- *If you must make a mistake with a lob, make it deep rather than short* (Diagram 15.9). Direct shots to the backcourt area by making the ball reach its peak near the opposite service line.
- *Use the lob more often when your opponent has to look into the sun.* If the other player tries to take part of the court away by coming to the net, take some of his or her vision away by putting the ball between him or her and the sun.

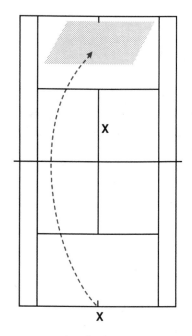

Diagram 15.9 Aim for the backcourt on lobs.

- *Hit most defensive lobs crosscourt* (Diagram 15.10). If you make a mistake and the ball does not go deep into the opponent's court, the angle of his return would be less if you hit crosscourt than it would be down-the-line. A short lob down-the-line gives the other player lots of space to hit a winning crosscourt smash.
- *Follow good offensive lobs to the net (stop at about the service line).* This puts pressure on your opponent to hit a good return. An offensive lob is as good as an approach shot. Use it to take the net from your opponent.
- *Lob at times just to make your opponent aware that your lob is a threat.* If you don't lob occasionally, opponents would play very close to the net without any fear of losing the point to a lob.
- *Lob high if you are in a defensive position.* Give yourself as much time as you can to recover, return to a central position, and have a chance to win the point.
- *Lob low when you are trying to win a point with the shot.* A perfect lob barely clears the net player's racket and does not allow

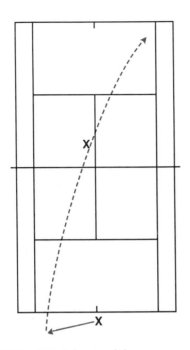

Diagram 15.10 Hit defensive lobs crosscourt.

time for that player to retreat for a return before the ball bounces twice.

- *Lob to the backhand if you can do it without risking an error.* One of the most difficult shots in tennis is the high backhand, so even if your opponent gets a racket on the shot, there is not much he or she can do with the return.

HOW TO USE THE SMASH

As you develop into a full-court player, the smash can become the shot that closes out the point. Otherwise, if you work hard to put yourself in a position to win but cannot put the finishing touch on the point, your work would be wasted. Focus on only one of the following suggestions at a time:

- *Smash after the bounce if you can do it without losing your offensive position.* Let the court take away the effects of spin and wind on the ball.
- *Do not let the ball bounce—hit it in the air— if you would lose your offensive position after the bounce.* Most offensive lobs have to be played in the air. If you let them bounce, you would have to retreat too far back for the next shot.

- *When close to the net, hit smashes flat.* You can hit flat shots with more power and with a higher bounce, making your opponent move back to the fence or wall for a return.
- *When in the backcourt area, hit smashes with spin.* The spin allows you to swing hard and still get the ball down and into the opponent's court.
- *Change the direction of a second consecutive smash.* If you hit the first smash of a point down the middle, hit the second at an angle. Open up the court by making your opponent move from side to side while chasing your smashes.
- *When you are close to the net, hit smashes at an angle* (Diagram 15.11). The forward position gives you more court to see clearly and less chance of making an error with the shot. Hitting at an angle means directing the shot so that the ball bounces inside the singles boundaries and exits the court by passing over either sideline. If your opponent has to run wide to retrieve the first smash, the court should be open for your next shot.

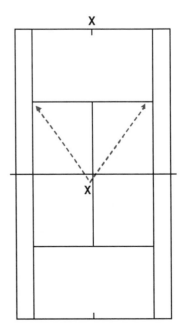

Diagram 15.11 Smash at an angle when close to the net.

- *Hit smashes deep and to a corner if you are deep in your backcourt*. You may win the point outright (although that is not the objective of a smash from this position). If not, you will be in great position to finish the point on the next shot. Be ready to move in following that shot for a winner.
- *Do not try to win the point with a smash if you are near your baseline*. There is too much distance for the ball to travel for it to be a winner. Hit the shot firmly and deeply, and wait for a shallow return for your put-away smash.

HOW TO USE THE DROP SHOT

Use the drop shot at least enough to keep your opponent honest. Let him or her know that you will use this shot. Don't overuse it, and follow these suggestions (one at a time) regarding drop shot strategy:

- *Try drop shots from the forecourt area*. If you attempt to hit a drop from the baseline, the ball stays in the air long enough for the opponent to get to it.
- *Use drop shots against slow-moving players*. Take advantage of their lack of speed.
- *Use drop shots against players who are in poor physical condition*. Make them pay for their weaknesses.
- *Do not try drop shots when there is a strong wind at your back*. The ball may carry to your opponent's midcourt area for a setup.
- *Do not try drop shots against players who can run fast*. They can turn good-looking shots into better-looking shots for themselves.

Singles Situation Drills

There are situations that occur repeatedly in singles play. The more you can practice such situations, the more confident and comfortable you will be when you see them under competitive conditions.

In these drills, start each point with the combination of shots described, then play the point out. Practice a situation 5 times, keep score, change roles with your practice partner, then play the next sequence of strokes.

1. Serve-Return Drill

Player A serves; player B returns the serve with a forehand or backhand groundstroke. Player A, keep the serve deep. Player B, prepare for hard serves with short backswings.

Success Goal = total of 10 serve-return points played out

  a. 5 serves

  b. 5 returns

Your Score =

  a. (#) _____ points won out of 5 attempts as player A

  b. (#) _____ points won out of 5 attempts as player B

2. Serve-Lob Drill

Player A serves; player B returns with a lob deep to the backhand corner.

Success Goal = total of 10 serve-lob points played out

  a. 5 serves

  b. 5 lobs

Your Score =

  a. (#) _____ points won out of 5 attempts as player A

  b. (#) _____ points won out of 5 attempts as player B

3. Serve–Short Return Drill

Player A serves; player B returns with a short shot to the open side of the court. Receiver, watch to see where the server stands to put the ball into play; and return to the side with the most open space. Watch the racket face to help anticipate the next shot.

Success Goal = total of 10 serve–short return points played out

  a. 5 serves

  b. 5 short returns

Your Score =

  a. (#) _____ points won out of 5 attempts as player A

  b. (#) _____ points won out of 5 attempts as player B

4. *Passing Shot Drill*

Player A drops a ball and hits down a line; player B starts from a volleying position and cuts the shot off at the net with a forehand or backhand volley. Player A, keep the ball low on passing shots. Player B, remember to move diagonally toward the net to cut off passing shots.

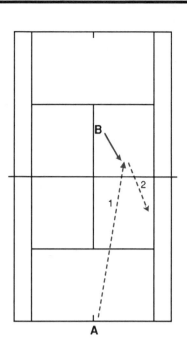

Success Goal = total of 10 passing shot points played out

   a. 5 down-the-line hits

   b. 5 cut-offs from the net

Your Score =

   a. (#) _____ points won out of 5 attempts as player A

   b. (#) _____ points won out of 5 attempts as player B

5. *Approach Drill*

Player A hits a short shot to one side of the forecourt; player B moves in and hits an approach shot down-the-line. Take shorter backswings on approach shots; because your weight is moving forward, avoid overhitting the ball.

Success Goal = total of 20 approach shots hit

   a. 10 short shots

   b. 10 approach shots

Your Score =

   a. (#) _____ short shots (setups) out of 10 attempts

   b. (#) _____ approach shots hit out of 10 attempts

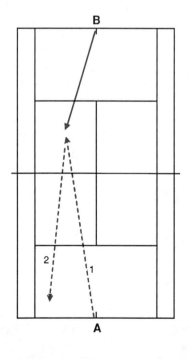

6. *Approach-Lob Drill*

Player A hits a short shot, player B moves in and hits an approach shot, and player A returns with a lob. Player A, hit the lob cross-court if you are driven deep into a corner.

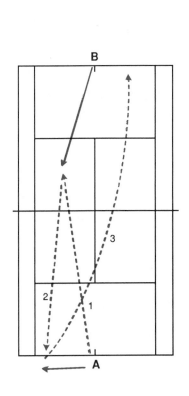

Success Goal = total of 10 approach-lob points played out

   a. 5 short shots, then lobs

   b. 5 approach shots

Your Score =

   a. (#) _____ points out of 5 attempts as player A

   b. (#) _____ points out of 5 attempts as player B

7. *Approach-Pass Drill*

Player A hits a short shot, player B moves in and hits an approach shot, and player A returns with a down-the-line groundstroke. Player B, follow your shot by moving closer to the net and staying on a line behind your shot and slightly toward the center of the court. Player A, don't try to pass with a cross-court shot unless you get to the ball early.

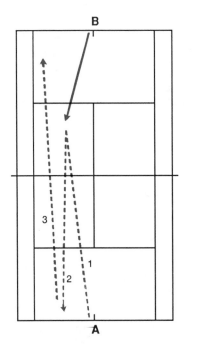

Success Goal = total of 10 approach-pass points played out

   a. 5 short shots, then down-the-line shots

   b. 5 approach shots

Your Score =

   a. (#) _____ points out of 5 attempts as player A

   b. (#) _____ points out of 5 attempts as player B

8. Attack-Lob Drill

Player A hits a forcing shot anywhere in the backcourt; player B returns with a lob. Lob deep, high, and preferably to the backhand side. Follow a good lob by moving in toward the service line to prepare for the return.

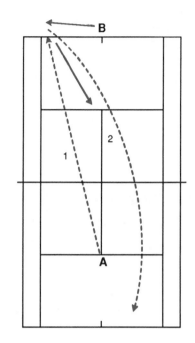

Success Goal = total of 10 attack-lob points played out

  a. 5 forcing shots

  b. 5 lobs

Your Score =

  a. (#) _____ points out of 5 attempts as player A

  b. (#) _____ points out of 5 attempts as player B

9. Lob-Smash Drill

Player A hits a lob; player B starts at the net and returns with a smash. Player B, retreat quickly if the lob is deep. Plant your back foot and lean forward as you hit the smash. Try to keep the ball in front of your body position.

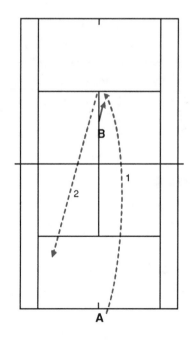

Success Goal = total of 10 lob-smash points played out

  a. 5 lobs

  b. 5 smashes

Your Score =

  a. (#) _____ points out of 5 attempts as player A

  b. (#) _____ points out of 5 attempts as player B

10. *Moon Ball Drill*

Players A and B hit consecutive lobs; the ball must bounce between the service line and the baseline. Keep the ball in play with a moon ball (a high, deep groundstroke) rally until someone makes a mistake by hitting a weak, short shot. Then finish the point with any stroke that will win it for you.

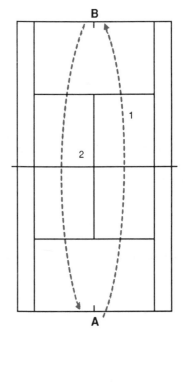

Success Goal = total of 10 points played out

Your Score =

   a. (#) _____ points won

   b. (highest #) _____ consecutive lobs

11. *Serve-Return-Attack Drill*

Player A serves; player B returns with a short shot; player A hits a forcing shot and advances to the net, trying to anticipate whether player B will try a lob or a passing shot.

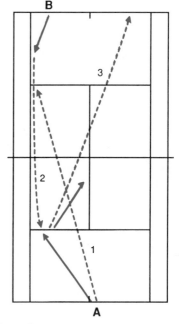

Success Goal = total of 10 serve-return-attack points played out

   a. 5 serve and advances

   b. 5 returns

Your Score =

   a. (#) _____ points out of 5 attempts as player A

   b. (#) _____ points out of 5 attempts as player B

12. Consecutive Volleys Drill

Players A and B take positions at opposite service lines and hit consecutive volleys. The point begins after 3 consecutive volleys have been exchanged. Return low shots back down the middle; hit high shots crosscourt for winners.

Success Goal = total of 10 consecutive volley points played out

Your Score = (#) _____ points won

13. Volley-Pass Drill

Player A volleys from the net while player B tries to pass player A with groundstrokes. The player at the net puts the ball into play so that the baseline player can hit a groundstroke from the middle of the baseline.

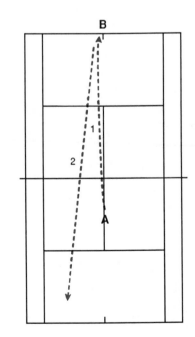

Success Goal = total of 10 volley-pass points played out
   a. 5 volleys
   b. 5 baseline groundstrokes

Your Score =
   a. (#) _____ points won out of 5 attempts as player A
   b. (#) _____ points won out of 5 attempts as player B

14. Lob-Retreat Drill

Player A takes a position at the net, player B lobs over A, and player A retreats to retrieve the lob. Player A, move back slightly to one side of the ball so you can return it with a forehand or backhand lob when you catch up with it.

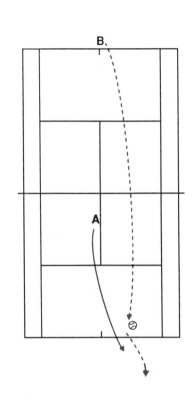

Success Goal = total of 10 lob-retreat points played out

    a. 5 retreats to retrieve lobs

    b. 5 lobs

Your Score =

    a. (#) _____ points won out of 5 attempts as player A

    b. (#) _____ points won out of 5 attempts as player B

15. Drop Shot–Lob Drill

Player A starts in the forecourt and puts the ball into play with a drop shot; player B moves forward and hits the ball back into player A's forecourt; player A lobs over player B's head. Player A, if player B gets to your drop shot, watch his or her racket face.

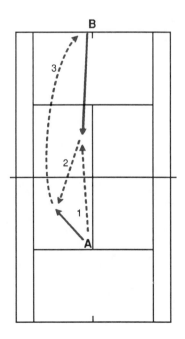

Success Goal = total of 10 drop shot–lob points played out

    a. 5 drop shots, then lobs

    b. 5 returns

Your Score =

    a. (#) _____ points won out of 5 attempts as player A

    b. (#) _____ points won out of 5 attempts as player B

GENERAL STRATEGY

Regardless of the stroke being used in singles, there are some general guidelines to keep in mind as you develop a game plan:

- Hit the simplest shot that will win the point.
- Use your best shot in crucial situations.
- Expect your opponent's best shot in crucial situations.
- In pressure situations, play the ball instead of your opponent.
- If you are having problems adjusting to a surface, get to the net more often.
- Slow the match down if you are losing a fast match.
- Aim for general target areas rather than lines.
- Do not try risky shots on critical points.
- Take chances on unimportant points (ones you can afford to lose).
- Try something different if you are losing.

Step 16 Using Your Strokes in Doubles

The selection of shots—when and how to use them—is one of the keys to successful doubles. Although speed, strength, and endurance may be more important in singles, factors such as judgment, shot placement, and anticipation can make average singles players excellent doubles players. Most tennis players become good doubles players long after they have achieved success in singles. You can get a head start in your development by following the suggestions below.

HOW TO USE GROUNDSTROKES

Groundstrokes are necessary, but less important in doubles than in singles. Good doubles players win with good serves, volleys, and smashes. Forehands and backhands from the baseline should be used as a means of getting into position to win points with more forceful shots.

- *Receive serves from a point approximately where the baseline meets the singles sideline* (Diagram 16.1). Because the server will probably put the ball into play from a position near the alley, compensate by moving to cover the angle of the serve.
- *Stand just inside the baseline against players with weak serves.* This puts you in a position to attack the serve and move toward the net.
- *If the server remains on the baseline following the serve, return the ball deep and crosscourt, then go to the net* (Diagram 16.2). This applies only if you are an intermediate or advanced player with a good net game.
- *If the server comes to the net following the serve, return the ball crosscourt and to the server's feet* (Diagram 16.3). This forces the server to volley the ball up, setting you and your partner up for a strong second shot.

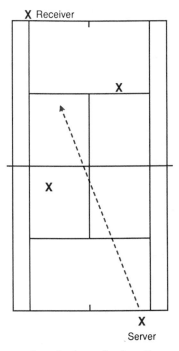

Diagram 16.1 Stand where the baseline meets the singles sideline to receive the serve.

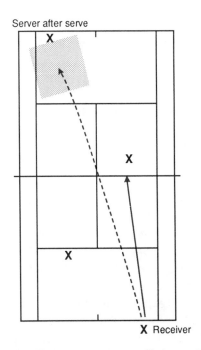

Diagram 16.2 Return crosscourt and deep, then approach the net if the server stays back (intermediate and advanced players).

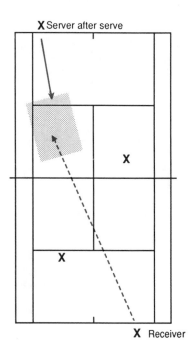

X Server after serve

X

X

X Receiver

Diagram 16.3 Return crosscourt and at the server's feet if the server comes to the net.

- *When you try to pass the server's partner at the net, aim for the singles sideline.* Leave a margin of error instead of trying to hit the doubles sideline.
- *Attempt to pass the net player occasionally, even if you lose the point.* It keeps that player honest and makes him or her wonder whether and when you will try the shot again.
- *When your partner is forced to move out of position, shift to cover the open court until your partner can recover* (Diagram 16.4). If you don't, your opponents will have an open space for their next shot.
- *Let the player on your team with the forehand take most of the shots that come down the middle.* Most players have stronger forehands than backhands.
- *When you and your partner are on the baseline and your opponents are at the net, hit most shots low and down the middle* (Diagram 16.5). Low shots make it difficult for the other team to hit winning volleys, and shots down the middle reduce the angle of opponents' returns and may create some confusion about who should make the shot.

- *Do not rely on groundstrokes to win in doubles.* Most doubles matches are won with serves, volleys, and smashes.

HOW TO USE THE SERVE

Placing the ball in specific locations becomes more important in doubles. Once you figure out where the other players are weak or which spots on the court they leave open, it is important to be able to hit those spots. This is a relatively sophisticated skill and one that requires a lot of practice. The main objective still is to get the ball in play, but putting it into play in the right places makes things easier for you and your partner.

- *Stand approximately halfway between the center mark and the doubles sideline to serve* (see Diagram 16.1). From this position you can cover the court from the middle to the alley when the return is made crosscourt. Your partner can cover the other half of the court on everything but lobs.
- *Serve at 3/4 speed deep to the backhand or to an open area.* The backhand is usually the weakest shot, putting the ball deep keeps the receiver from attacking your serve, and hitting at 3/4 speed is safe. It also allows you more time to get to the net following the serve.
- *Serve wide to the right-hander's backhand in the odd (left) court.* The combination of the wide serve and your partner being positioned at the net reduces the possibility of a good return.
- *Serve wide to the left-hander's backhand in the even (right) court.* A left-hander should not be playing that side, but take advantage of it if he or she is.
- *Let the stronger server begin serving each set.* The order of serve may be changed with each set, so use the rule to start out with a strong serve.
- *Serve down the middle if your partner is good at poaching, moving across to volley the return of serve.* A serve down the middle almost has to be returned down the middle and, therefore, can be anticipated for a winning volley.

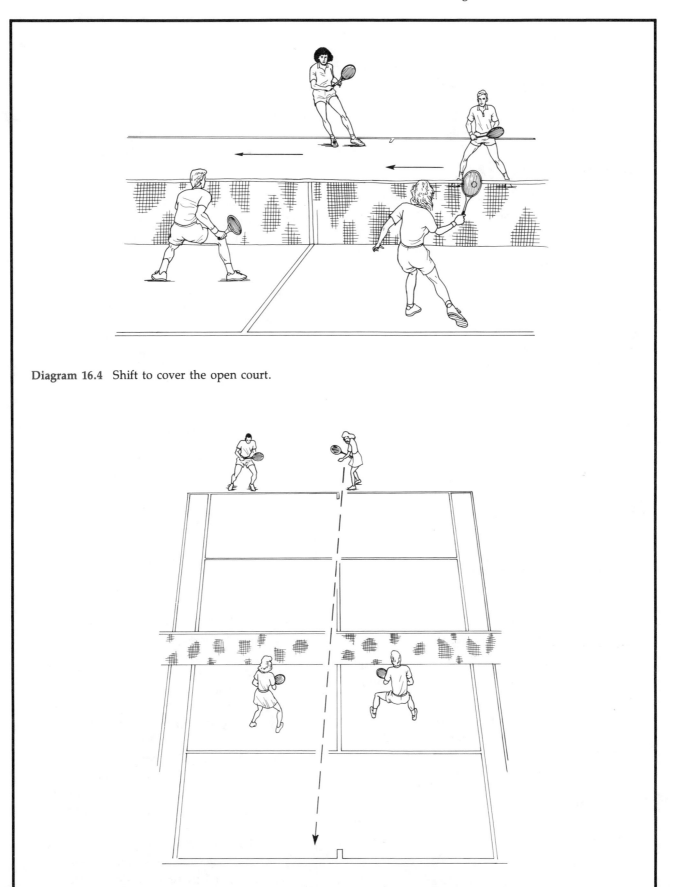

Diagram 16.4 Shift to cover the open court.

Diagram 16.5 Hit low and down the middle when your opponents are at the net.

Use more spin on serves to give yourself time to get to the net. A hard, flat serve may sound like a good idea; if the ball comes back, though, it comes before you have time to reach a good volleying position.

HOW TO USE THE LOB

Although the lob is not a primary weapon in doubles, it certainly should be an integral part of a good doubles team's collection of shots. Having a variety of shots and knowing when to use them can offset the power game of aggressive doubles opponents.

- *If you lob, lob over the player closer to the net, then follow your lob to the net*. When you move forward following the lob, stop at the service line. If your opponent puts up a weak, shallow return, there is still time to move in farther for a winning smash or volley. If the return is lobbed back deeper into your court, the service line position allows you to hit a smash without having to retreat.
- *Use the offensive lob if the net player poaches often*. The net player's partner will get tired of chasing down balls on the other side of the court.
- *When in doubt, lob deep and down the center of the court*. Almost every doubles shot hit toward the center is a good percentage shot.

HOW TO USE THE SMASH

An effective smash in doubles is not just important—it is essential. If the other team figures out that either you or your partner cannot hit winning smashes, watch out! Because every serving point begins with one player at the net, that person will be tested early to see what happens on a lob to that side. Also, because the idea in doubles is to take the net away from the other team as early in a point as possible, that strategy will not work if you cannot finish the point with a winning smash.

- *Smash the first lob to the outside of your opponent's court to open up the court*. Once a player has to move wide to retrieve a ball,

that player's partner will have trouble covering all of the remaining open space on the court.
- *Smash down the middle if it is open, in order to create confusion about which partner should return the shot*. The smashes should be low if both opponents are at the net, and high if they are in the backcourt. Once they move to the middle to protect against the shot, you may have another opening or two to the outside.
- *Let the partner with the stronger smash take overheads down the middle*. Don't dominate the court if you have the better smash, but work out a system to take advantage of each partner's strengths.
- *In advanced levels of tennis, hit smashes at players in weak positions*. Do not hit to hurt anyone, but don't give away points trying to be nice.

HOW TO USE THE VOLLEY

Remember that good doubles players can serve to specific spots in the service courts and follow these serves with volleys. The team that gets to the net first in doubles controls the outcome of the point. On the return of serve, if you can chip the ball short or drive it crosscourt and deep, and then follow your shot to the net, your team can finish the point with strong volleys.

- *When your partner is serving, stand about 8–12 feet from the net and two or three steps inside the singles sideline (see Diagram 16.1)*. From this position you can cut off weak returns without giving up too much space for a return down the alley. You are also in a good position to poach.
- *When your partner serves wide, shift slightly toward the alley*. You can cover the sideline and alley area, and your partner can cover the middle of the court. Tempt the other team to try to pass your partner with a crosscourt shot.
- *When your partner is serving, protect your side of the court, take weak shots down the middle, and smash any lobs hit to your side of the court unless your partner calls for the shot*. Your

job is much more than just protecting the alley. You actually have as much court to cover as your partner; only the starting position is different.

- *In quick exchanges at the net, the last player to hit a shot should take the next shot if it comes down the middle.* Establishing this agreement between partners can avoid confusion that may lead to no one hitting the ball.
- *When your partner is serving, tempt the receiver to try a shot down your alley.* If he or she can't hit that spot, move even farther away from the alley. If you get beaten more than once by leaving that part of the court open, close it by moving back.
- *Go for a winner when you poach.* It is not a defensive shot. If you don't win the point with that shot, either get back to your original position or continue to the other side so your partner will know where to go. If your first volley doesn't win the point, part of the court will be left open until you and your partner recover.
- *Poach occasionally, even if you lose the point.* Make the other team aware of the threat of the poach.
- *Poach more often when your partner is serving well.* Avoid poaching if your partner is weak with the serve.
- *Poach less often if your partner has a good volley.* Don't take away a player's best shot by moving in front and cutting the ball off.
- *Fake the poach at times.* It gives the other team one more thing to worry about.
- *During rallies, look at the racket faces of your opponents.* Do not turn and look to see what your partner is doing. You may get hit in the face, and you will lose a split second in reaction time when you turn back to your opponents.
- *Play farther from the net against players who lob frequently.* You can take away some of their lobbing space.
- *Play closer to the net against players who seldom lob.* Take anything they are willing to give you.

- *Retreat quickly, then take a defensive position when your opponents are set up for a smash.* Don't get hurt. Get as far back as you can before the shot, then dig in, stay low, and put the racket in front of your body. You may be able to deflect the ball back after the smash. Lucky shots count just as much as good shots.
- *Stand farther from the net if your partner's serve is weak.* You may need the extra time to react to the return of the serve.
- *Shift slightly with every shot to cover the open court.* Keep moving. Make your opponents think about your position. If you stay in one place, the other team can gang up against your partner without worrying about you.
- *Play farther from the net than usual if you are a stronger player than your partner.* You may be able to take shots that he or she cannot handle. If you are weaker than your partner, play closer to the net; this way you can give your partner more shots and more opportunities to set you up for winning volleys.

HOW TO USE DROP SHOTS

Although there may be exceptions, using drop shots in doubles is not a very good idea. If you do use one, wait until your opponents are pushed deep and out of position, then hit to the side of the slower player.

MIXED DOUBLES

In social mixed doubles, there are some unwritten rules. Those rules are mostly don'ts, such as (a) don't deliberately smash a setup directly at the weaker partner; (b) don't hit too many shots at the weaker partner; and (c) don't try to intimidate the weaker player on a team by hitting hard shots at that player, especially when he or she is at the net. The idea of social mixed doubles is for everyone to have a good time, to get into the action, and to come away from the match in good physical and emotional health.

In tournament competition, however, these rules do not apply. Competitive mixed doubles should be played exactly like men's and women's doubles.

Serves should be hit with proper velocity, and to the place in the service court most likely to produce a winning point, regardless of the receiver's gender. Shots should be directed to the weaker player if the situation calls for that shot. Each player—man and woman—should cover his or her side of the court. The man should not cut in front of his partner unless percentage tennis would dictate the same tactic in men's doubles. If the man poaches too often or hogs groundstrokes, he weakens his team's position by leaving part of the court open for the return. He also demeans his partner. He should pay for both offenses.

Given the level of men's and women's tennis today, playing mixed doubles probably means that the team with the stronger woman will win. This is especially true if this woman can play well at the net. In the past, women have been hesitant about developing a net game, but that has changed.

Positioning in mixed doubles should depend on which side of the court each partner can play best. There are some people who believe that the crucial points are played on the ad court and the stronger partner should line up on that side when the other team serves. Even if this is true, the advantage of having each player play from the side on which he or she is most effective and comfortable outweighs the crucial point theory.

Because mixed doubles usually has the least priority in practice and playing time, use as many shots as you can that create teamwork problems between opposing partners. Moving the ball around the court as much as possible is a good way to manipulate the other team. Lobs are especially effective because one player has to give way to the other, or the partners have to change positions on the court before hitting. Drop shots are usually not a good idea in doubles, but they work in mixed doubles to move opponents out of position and to open an area for a winning shot.

Finally, make the opposing mixed doubles team do what its members do not want to do. If either player is shy about playing the net, make that player come to the net by hitting short shots. If the team is very aggressive and likes coming to the net, use the lob to keep the partners off-balance. If one partner wants to dominate, make that player get out of position to do it. If the partners are not used to playing together, hit a lot of shots down the middle to create confusion about who should play the ball.

Take mixed doubles seriously. There are very few good teams, so the road to the top may be easier for you and your partner than in singles and doubles. Age and experience on the same team are as important as youth and strength, so a good team can keep on winning for a long time.

Doubles Situation Drills

Just as repetition can help you refine tennis strokes, it can also help you develop your ability to use those strokes in game situations. Following are drills to simulate doubles situations. Players A and C comprise one team; players B and D comprise the other. Practice each situation 5 times, then rotate so that each player begins points at every position on the court.

1. Serve-Return-Poach Drill

Player A serves; player B returns; player C poaches and volleys to the open court or to player D at the opposite service line.

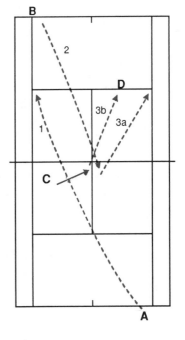

Success Goal = total of 10 points played

  a. 5 serves, then poaches

  b. 5 returns

Your Score =

  a. (#) _____ points won out of 5 attempts as players A and C

  b. (#) _____ points won out of 5 attempts as players B and D

2. Serve-Lob Drill

Player A serves; player B returns with a lob over player C at the net; player C smashes or moves to cover the other side of the court.

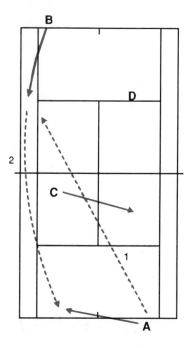

Success Goal = total of 10 points played

    a. 5 serves, then smashes

    b. 5 lobs

Your Score =

    a. (#) _____ points won out of 5 attempts as players A and C

    b. (#) _____ points won out of 5 attempts as players B and D

3. Continuous Volleys Drill

Players A, B, C, and D exchange continuous volleys from positions near the service line. The point does not begin until 3 volleys have been exchanged.

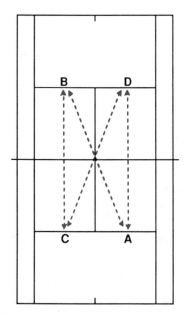

Success Goal = total of 10 points played

Your Score = (#) _____ points won

4. *Serve-Crosscourt Return Drill*

Player A serves; player B returns crosscourt past player C at the net.

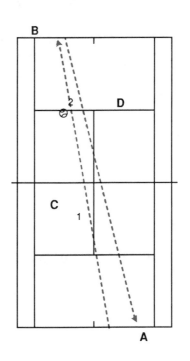

Success Goal = total of 10 points played

   a. 5 serves

   b. 5 crosscourt returns

Your Score =

   a. (#) _____ points won out of 5 attempts as players A and C

   b. (#) _____ points won out of 5 attempts as players B and D

5. *Serve-Return-Drive Drill*

Player A serves; player B returns crosscourt; player A hits the third shot with a forcing groundstroke.

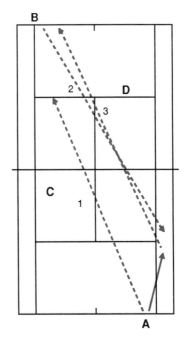

Success Goal = total of 10 points played

   a. 5 serves, then forcing groundstrokes

   b. 5 crosscourt returns

Your Score =

   a. (#) _____ points won out of 5 attempts as players A and C

   b. (#) _____ points won out of 5 attempts as players B and D

6. Serve–Forcing Return Drill

Player A serves to player B; player B returns with a forcing shot and advances to the net with D.

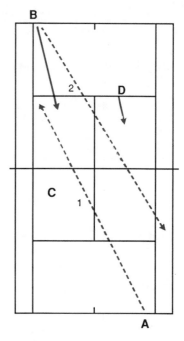

Success Goal = total of 10 points played

   a. 5 serves

   b. 5 returns

Your Score =

   a. (#) _____ points won out of 5 attempts as players A and C

   b. (#) _____ points won out of 5 attempts as players B and D

7. Two-on-Two Rallies Drill

Players A and C stand at one baseline and hit groundstrokes to B and D, who stand at the net and hit volleys. The point does not begin until 3 shots have been exchanged.

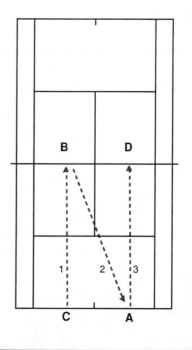

Success Goal = total of 10 points played

Your Score = (#) _____ points won

8. Two-on-One Groundstroke Volley Drill

With only three players, A and C hit ground-strokes from the baseline to B, who tries to win points with volleys at the net. The point does not begin until 3 shots have been exchanged.

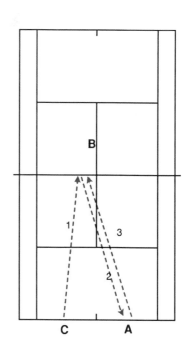

Success Goal = total of 15 points played

Your Score =

    a. (#) _____ points won out of 5 attempts as player A

    b. (#) _____ points won out of 5 attempts as player B

    c. (#) _____ points won out of 5 attempts as player C

9. One-on-Two Groundstroke-Volley Drill

With three players, A hits shots from the base-line to B and C who stand near the net and try to win points with volleys. The point does not begin until 3 shots have been exchanged.

Success Goal = total of 15 points played

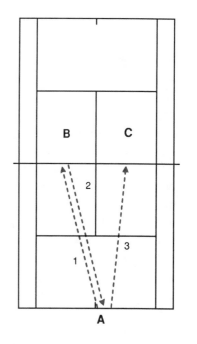

Your Score =

    a. (#) _____ points won out of 5 attempts as player A

    b. (#) _____ points won out of 5 attempts as player B

    c. (#) _____ points won out of 5 attempts as player C

10. Two-on-One Lob-Smash Drill

With three players, A and C lob to B, who tries to win points with smashes, which A and C retrieve and lob.

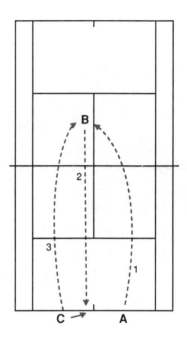

Success Goal = total of 15 points played

Your Score =

   a. (#) _____ points won out of 5 attempts as player A

   b. (#) _____ points won out of 5 attempts as player B

   c. (#) _____ points won out of 5 attempts as player C

GENERAL STRATEGY

In addition to shot selection and practicing situations to improve as a doubles player, consider these ideas:

- Don't assume that a good singles player is necessarily a good doubles player.
- Play with someone you like.
- Play with someone who does not criticize you after a bad shot.
- Play with someone who complements your game (whose strengths compensate for your weaknesses).
- Accept your role as part of a team; don't try to dominate the action.
- Left-handers and right-handers usually make good doubles partners. Whatever you are, look for the other one.

- Communicate with your partner.
- Stay out of the middle of the court (no-man's-land) as much as possible.
- Be more aggressive than normal if your partner is much weaker than you.
- Unless you play regularly with the same partner, learn to play the left and right sides when receiving serves.
- Protect the middle more than the alleys in doubles.
- When you go for winners, hit to the corners of the singles court.
- Force the action in doubles. Make something good happen instead of waiting for something to happen.

Step 17 Adjusting to Opponents and Conditions

As if you didn't have enough tennis challenges to master already, there are still more variables that affect your play. There are different kinds of players, court surfaces, and weather conditions. The ability to adjust to each one can make a difference in whether you win or lose. There are no drills in this step because it is difficult to simulate playing the players and conditions discussed. However, here are some suggestions that may help you make those adjustments, when needed.

PLAYING AGAINST BIG HITTERS

Big hitters (players who rely on power) usually have heavy, flat serves, hard groundstrokes, put-away volleys, and big overhead smashes. These opponents like to serve and rush the net. Their asset is power. Their weaknesses, though, may be lack of patience, mobility, and consistency; it is difficult to hit consistently big shots for an entire match. Watch for these weaknesses and be ready to take advantage of them. Most of all, don't be intimidated. These people can be beaten, even if they look better than you do while they are losing.

- Play a step or two deeper on service returns.
- Shorten your backswing on all shots.
- Do not fight power with power.
- Slow the match down; play at your pace, not your opponent's.
- Keep the ball deep to prevent the big hitter from constantly attacking.
- Accept being overpowered occasionally; don't let it affect the next point.
- Hit some shots directly at the power player who takes a big windup.

PLAYING AGAINST RETRIEVERS

It can be very frustrating to play retrievers—players who get everything back, but with little pace. They are certainly not intimidating players, and they probably won't impress you with their strokes. If you watch them warm up or play against someone else, it is easy to become overconfident.

The problem is that the ball seems to keep coming back over the net from them no matter how well you are playing. These players know their capabilities and their weaknesses, and they play within their limitations. This ability is one that all tennis players could use. Here are some ideas on how to play these "human backboards."

- Make the retriever come to the net; he or she is not comfortable there.
- Occasionally try to overpower the retriever.
- Attack the second serve.
- Avoid playing the retriever's style of tennis; play *your* game.
- Respect the retriever as much as any other kind of opponent. Looking impressive and hitting hard is not as important as winning matches.
- If you have a choice, avoid playing a retriever on a slow court; he or she is made for that kind of slow, get-everything-back style of play.

PLAYING AGAINST LEFT-HANDERS

Left-handers have a tremendous advantage in tennis. No one is used to playing them, and few people enjoy playing against them. Every crucial shot seems to go to the left-hander's forehand. It takes almost a set to figure out the left-hander's serve. The only group of players who dislike them more than right-handers is other left-handers; it disrupts their games, too.

Left-handers may be discriminated against in society, but on the tennis court they are an elite minority. The number of successful left-handed players seems to be disproportionately high compared to the number playing the game. Try these strategies to overcome their natural advantages:

- Regroove your strokes to avoid hitting to the forehand side.
- From the right side, serve wide to the left-hander's backhand.
- Serve down the middle most of the time from the ad court.
- Expect the left-hander's serve to spin to your left.
- In quick exchanges and on crucial points, remember that your normal put-away shots might go to the left-hander's strength.

PLAYING ON FAST COURTS

Good tennis players can adjust to any kind of surface, but going to a fast, slick court from any other kind of court is particularly difficult because the ball skids and takes a low bounce on slick courts. If you have to make such an adjustment, try to schedule some practice time on the court before match day. The entire pace of the game is faster on a fast court. Shots seem to be hit harder, rallies are shorter, and there is less time to get into the rhythm of the match. Try these tactics:

- Draw your racket back early and start your swing earlier than you would normally.
- Play deeper than usual, especially on the return of serve.
- Go to the net on shots that you would not normally follow.
- Expect your opponent to be more aggressive than on slow courts.
- Be conscious of bending your knees and staying low to hit groundstrokes.
- Don't overhit setups; the fast court provides some pace to your shots.

PLAYING ON SLOW COURTS

The adjustment to a slow court is much easier than it is to a fast court when you are not accustomed to such a surface. On rough courts, the ball slows down and bounces higher than on fast courts. Instead of having less time to prepare for shots, there is more than enough time on a slow court. The problems you face are not being able to put shots away as easily, and becoming impatient because the points last longer. Retrievers love these courts, and power players hate them. Everyone else can win a few more points by trying this strategy:

- Be more deliberate than on a fast court; careful shot selection and placement is very important.
- Be patient; it takes time to win on a slow court.
- Do not waste energy trying to serve aces.
- Be careful about advancing to the net.
- Do not underestimate the retriever on a slow court.
- Stay in good physical condition if you play most of your matches on slow courts; points, games, sets, and matches take longer to complete.

PLAYING IN THE WIND

There are two ways to approach the problems created by playing in the wind. The first is to dread the whole experience, complain about conditions, and blame poor play or losses on windy conditions. The other approach is to try to use the wind to your advantage. It can keep shots in the court that would normally go out, it can add pace to average or weak shots, and it can cause more trouble for your opponent than for you. The trick is to become so involved in the match that you don't even worry about the wind.

- Let wind at your back provide some of the power on your strokes.
- Consider choosing to play against the wind in the first game of a match.
- Toss the ball lower on the serve.
- Keep lobbing to a minimum, especially against the wind.

- Play closer to the net when the wind is against you.
- Play more aggressively when the wind is against you.

PLAYING IN HOT WEATHER

Prepare for playing in extreme heat as if preparing to play a tough opponent. Don't ignore the problems hot weather can create. Players who try to prove how tough they are run the risks of cramps, dehydration, fatigue, and not being able to hold onto the racket during long points.

- Do not wear yourself out trying to hit hard serves.

- Try to make your opponent move around the court more than in cooler weather.
- Keep your racket handle dry with towels, wrist bands, sawdust, or other drying agents, and by alternating rackets during a match.
- Alternate rackets (if you have more than one) every time you change ends of the court.
- Dress comfortably and coolly.
- Take water to the court and drink it often.
- Stay in the shade as much as possible between points and games.
- Wear a hat.
- Use a sunscreen.

Step 18 Concentration

Concentration means directing attention to a single task or object. In tennis the task is to play the game as well as possible, and the object is the tennis ball. There are many natural and man-made distractions that can prevent players from concentrating on either the game or the ball.

Before getting too involved in trying to reach a higher level of concentration, be sure you want to. There are thousands of players who just want to go out, hit the ball, have a good time, and not worry about directing total attention all of the time to the game being played. There is a great enjoyment in talking with friends, being out-of-doors, watching others play, and generally relaxing.

However, if you are intent on becoming highly skilled, competitive, and very serious about tennis, there are some problems and solutions when it comes to concentration. The key is to block out as much unnecessary stuff as possible from your mind, leaving only the game to think about. Obviously, this is almost impossible when you consider that tennis matches usually last 1–3 hours; nobody has an attention span that long. So, the goal becomes one of mentally eliminating as many distractions as possible while on the court. First, consider some of the distractions that are around the court.

PEOPLE

People can be a major hindrance to your concentration. There are people on the adjacent courts who are talking, playing, hitting balls onto your court, and occasionally getting in your way or in your field of vision. Ignore them as much as you can without being discourteous. Do not watch their matches, even if their matches are more interesting than yours. Do not try to keep up with their scores. Play your own match. If your curiosity gets the best of you, get it out of your system by asking what the score is at a time when you will not interrupt their match.

There may also be people in the stands or near your court watching your match. Keep your eyes out of the stands. Some players find it difficult to keep from glancing around to see who saw that last shot. If you are "counting the house," you are not concentrating on what is happening on your court.

Even the people on your own court can hinder your concentration. Some players may deliberately try to distract you or interrupt your thinking with an assortment of gamesmanship maneuvers. Some of the more popular methods of distraction are stalling instead of playing continuously, talking to you or to spectators, being overly dramatic after a point has been completed, and giving you a bad call just to upset you.

There are two ways to handle these situations without totally losing concentration. The first is to decide that nothing an opponent can do will bother you. If you expect trouble from an opponent or even if you get it unexpectedly, you must make a conscious decision to retain your poise and concentration regardless of what happens. This is a difficult task, and it becomes even more difficult if you are losing. Then, even minor irritations become magnified. It is a lot easier to concentrate when you are winning than when you are getting beat.

If a nonaggression policy does not work, then you might as well confront the person who is bothering you and try to solve the problem before the match continues. There is no use putting up with distractions if you are going to let worrying about them interfere with your game; if you are thinking about the problems, you are not thinking about tennis. Stop the match, call your opponent to the net, and state what is bothering you. If you don't get any cooperation, ask for an umpire or get a ruling from the tournament referee, if there is one. If the match is supposed to be merely a social one, do a better job of selecting opponents. It would be better to walk off the court than to become so incensed that an incident or loss of friendship might occur.

SUPERIOR OPPONENTS

Once a match begins, try not to worry too much about how good your opponent is. Even if he or she is great, you are stuck with each other, and it is best to go ahead and play your kind of game. If you walk around on tiptoes or fear that every shot by your opponent will be a winner, you will play below your capability. If you can relax a little and play each point rather than worry about the outcome of the match, you may play even better than you normally do. Superior players frequently bring out the best in inferior opponents.

WEAK OPPONENTS

On the other hand, do not let your mind wander if you are playing someone whom you should easily beat. Be nice, but try just as hard on every point as you would against someone who is your equal on the court. If you can win 6–0, do it. Never throw points or games in a match because you feel sorry for the person on the other side of the net. If an opponent cannot challenge your tennis skills, make the match a challenge to your concentration. Save your compassion for social tennis.

NOISE

Noise can be a distraction if you are not used to playing where the noise level is high. If people are making enough noise to warrant a legitimate complaint, either tolerate it or ask the people to be quieter. If the noise is coming from traffic, from work being done near the courts, or from passersby, learn to live with the noise or choose a quieter place to play. Actually, once you learn to play with a lot of noise, your concentration should improve. If you can concentrate when it is noisy,

you can surely concentrate better in quiet surroundings. Players who learn to play on public courts probably have an advantage over club players in this respect.

WIND

Some players allow the weather, especially the wind, to interfere with concentration. The solution to this problem may be to make it a point to practice as much as possible when it is windy. If you can adapt your game to windy conditions instead of worrying about them, this is one less obstacle to concentrating on your game.

EMOTIONAL DISTRACTIONS

In spite of all these outside distractions, most concentration problems come from within our own heads. We let our thoughts drift; we think about families, jobs, or studies; we worry about people seeing us make a bad shot; and we think about a thousand other things.

Because it is impossible to cut out all non-tennis thoughts, at least try to eliminate the obvious ones. First, play 1 point at a time. Try to remember that your opponent is not likely to hit any shot that you have not at least seen before this match. In fact, you have probably returned every type of shot he or she has to offer. You might see those shots more often or in different situations, but there aren't that many surprises out there. All the other player can do is hit groundstrokes, serves, volleys, lobs, and smashes. If you are overmatched, try to win points. If you can win a few points, you can win a game; and if you can win 1 game, you can probably win some more.

PLANNING POINTS

Have a plan on each point. Do not just wait to see what happens. You should know after a while where you want to place the ball, what your opponent does best, what he or she has trouble doing, and where you want to be on the court. If you are playing somebody better than you, you may not be able to carry out your plan. Yet, at least start with a plan, even if it is only to keep the ball in play as long as possible.

SELF-TALK

Avoid unnecessary talking. Too many players moan, groan, curse, shout, reprimand themselves, coach themselves, and even appeal to heaven for help. If you are talking about a point, you are probably talking about one that has already been completed and one that you can do nothing about. Instead of dwelling on the last point, think about the next one: Where am I going to hit the serve? Where is my opponent going to serve? Am I fresh enough to get to the net? Should I take it easy on this point? Do I play conservatively or aggressively on the next shot?

TALKING TO YOUR OPPONENT

Also avoid talking to your opponent. Don't be rude, but do not get carried away with compliments after good shots or chatting during side changes. The more you compliment other players, the more confident they become. They might begin to believe that they are as good as you keep telling them they are.

The more you chat during breaks, the less time you have to prepare yourself mentally for the next game. If you really want to concentrate, 99% of your talking during a match should consist of giving the score and calling shots out. Never call shots ''good'' or ''in'' during the point—just hit the ball.

PERSISTENCE

Do not give up after a bad shot. You are in the point until the ball goes into the net, goes out-of-bounds, or bounces twice. Some players stop thinking and trying when the opponent has a setup. Make your opponent put the ball away. Do not concede anything. Your opponent could blow an easy shot and you could retrieve a would-be winner. Tenacity is a sign that you are concentrating, and it can be demoralizing to the other player. Do not give up after you have lost a point.

Games, sets, and matches can take a long time to complete. Every player is going to lose points, miss setups, and occasionally be embarrassed by a good opponent. You have too many problems during a match to be worrying about how bad you look on 1 or 2 shots. Your time for the super shot will come if you have the patience to wait for it. A few bad points are part of the game; do not let them get you down.

PRACTICING

Concentration should improve if you practice as seriously as you play matches. Try to follow the suggestions presented in this book every time you walk onto the courts. If you can develop the ability to block out distractions during practice sessions, concentrating in matches should be easier because you have fewer outside distractions, greater motivation to play well, and better rewards if you win. Characteristics such as steadiness, poise, tenacity, silence, and concentration can be learned just as strokes can be learned. We do not inherit tennis behavior; we learn to act and think the way we do on the court.

PRIORITIES

Now, what should you think about during a match? Because people can only direct their attention to one thing at a time, a priority of thoughts has to be established. At the top of the list is the tennis ball. ''Keep your eye on the ball'' should be more than a platitude. If you are serving, try to watch the ball until it leaves your racket strings. If you are receiving the serve, focus on the ball while it is still in the tossing hand of the server. Follow it with your eyes from the toss to the point of contact, across the net, and into your racket. Do not worry about whether the serve is in or out until after you have swung at the ball. There is no penalty for calling a shot out after you hit it. Continue concentrating on the ball throughout the point; watch it while you and your opponent are preparing to hit, as well as hitting.

The second item on the concentration priority list is your opponent. As the ball leaves your racket, you have a second or two to watch where your opponent is on the court and how he or she is going to hit the next shot. The place to give special attention to is the face of the other player's racket. If you watch anything else except the racket and the ball, you can be faked out of position. Immediately after the ball is hit for the return to you, be aware of where your opponent is going to be on the court.

In this situation, your mind has to move rapidly back and forth between priority items. You have to be observant enough to know whether the other player is coming to the net, returning to the center of the baseline, or moving to one side of the court. Within a split second, your attention must again return to the ball.

The third item on your think list is your method of hitting the ball. You are much better off if you automatically move into the proper position rather than have to think about it. Because preparation for a stroke happens at the same time you are trying to concentrate on the ball, you cannot literally think about both things simultaneously. If your strokes are grooved to the point of thoughtless but effective preparation, you can devote full attention to the ball.

As if trying to direct attention to the ball, your opponent, and your own form is not enough, there are other factors worthy of your attention. The score in the game, the set score, the weather, your physical condition, your opponent's condition, and your game plan are all worth thinking about during a match. The time to do such thinking is between points and games, not while the ball is in play.

Become as totally absorbed in the match you are playing as possible. Try to isolate your playing from the rest of your life for the short period of time you are on the court. Forget for a while that there are many other things in your life more important than playing a game. If you can (and want to), create a temporary attitude in which the next point, game, or set is more important than family, friends, or society. It is doubtful that you can accomplish this, but if you set this standard as a goal, any progress toward this attitude should improve your game by improving your concentration.

Concentration Drills

1. Silent Practice Drill

Practice with a partner for 15 minutes without saying a word. Allow nothing to distract you from hitting the ball. Agree ahead of time on the practice routine to be followed. Any combination of strokes could be used, but 5 minutes of groundstrokes, 5 minutes of volleys, and 5 minutes of serves and returns is an example.

Variation: Increase the length of the silent practice by increments of 5 minutes each day.

Success Goal = 15 minutes of hitting without talking

Your Score = (#) _____ minutes

2. Silent Set Drill

Play an entire set without talking, except to call out the score when you are serving.

Success Goal = 1 set completed without talking

Your Score = (#) _____ games (or sets) completed

3. Jam Box Tennis Drill

Take a radio or jam box to the courts and play a match against an understanding friend (only when there are no other players to distract). Turn the radio or tape deck up louder than normal while you are playing the match. Try to maintain a high concentration level despite the added noise.

Success Goal = 1 match completed with the added noise

Your Score = (#) _____ sets completed

4. Take-Your-Best-Shot Drill

Play 10 points in which you set up your practice partner with his or her favorite, can't-miss, finish-the-point shot. Then play the point out. Keep score, then reverse roles to check your concentration and effectiveness when you are expected to finish points with your favorite shot.

Success Goal = total of 20 points played
   a. 2 points won out of 10 attempts
   b. 8 points won out of 10 attempts

Your Score =
   a. (#) _____ points won when you set up
   b. (#) _____ points won when you are set up

5. 0–40 Game

Play a set in which every game is started with the score 40–0 or 0–40 against you. Test your ability to maintain concentration and poise by coming from behind.

Success Goal = 1 game won in the set

Your Score = (#) _____ games won

6. Obstacle Course Tennis Drill

Play a set with four harmless obstacles (small boxes, rolled-up towels, racket covers) placed on your side of the court. Put one in each service court and two in the backcourt area. Hit your strokes without being distracted by the obstacles on the court. If your opponent hits an obstacle, you lose the point.

Success Goal = 1 set completed with the obstacles on your court

Your Score = (#) _____ sets

7. Plan-a-Point Drill

Plan a point in your mind, then try to play it out against an opponent in a practice set. For example, ''I will serve wide to the backhand, pulling him off the court; he will return short to my backhand; and I will finish the point with a crosscourt backhand to the open part of the court.'' Or, ''She will serve to my backhand, I will return short to force her to come to the net and hit an approach shot, and I will lob to her backhand corner and follow the shot to the net.''

Success Goal = executing at least 1 planned point in each game played

Your Score = (#) _____ points planned and executed during the set

8. Goal-Setting Drill

During a practice set, establish goals to improve your concentration. Give yourself 1 point every time a goal is reached during a set. Write down or mentally record the number of points earned when changing sides of the court. Select from the following examples and/or create your own goals.

Success Goal =

a. holding serve 3 times in one set

b. no double faults in a set

c. winning a game on the first game point

d. winning the first point of at least 4 games in a set

e. returning 1 shot no one would expect you to return in a set

f. breaking your opponent's serve once in a set

g. no points lost failing to return serve

h. _____

i. _____

Your Score =

a. (#) _____ serves held (1 point possible if goal reached)

b. (#) _____ double faults (1 point possible with no double faults)

c. (#) _____ games won on first game point (1 point possible)

d. (#) _____ first points won (1 point possible)

e. (#) _____ shots returned (1 point possible)

f. (#) _____ serves broken (1 point possible)

g. (#) _____ points lost (1 point possible if goal reached)

h. (#) _____

i. (#) _____

Step 19 **Learning by Watching**

Most people watch tennis matches because they can be entertaining, but you can also watch to improve your game and to scout future opponents. If you are interested in watching for either of those reasons, there are ways to get more out of your spectating.

WHERE TO WATCH

With all of the tennis being played today, there are many places to watch good players. Professional tournaments, television, college and high school matches, and local or regional tournaments all provide settings to improve your game by watching someone else play.

Of these four places to watch, professional tournaments are probably the least beneficial for the spectator who wants to learn. Professional players are so skilled and so gifted athletically, they cannot be compared to the average beginning or intermediate player. Many of the professionals have peculiarities in their styles of play that would not be appropriate as examples for lesser players. There are also too many distractions at pro tournaments. A person who goes to one of these events pays a lot of money to be entertained. There are celebrities to see, friends to talk with, scores to keep, things to buy, and many other sideshows to keep a person from carefully watching the mechanics of stroke production or court strategy. It is not impossible to learn by watching the pros—it is just very difficult. They provide more inspiration than instruction.

Televised matches offer a slightly better chance to learn how to play tennis, but there are still drawbacks. There are fewer distractions for the viewer, but the nature of television makes observation of many aspects of the game almost impossible. Watching a small screen, it is hard to get an accurate perspective on things like the velocity of the ball, trajectory, spin, or size and speed of the players. Everything seems to be miniaturized so much that the subtle aspects of the game are lost to many fans and players. You can also become so interested in who is winning and losing that nothing else is observed.

The best two places to learn by watching are probably at matches between good college teams and at tournaments in your area that attract outstanding amateur players. The quality of play is good enough to learn something, the players are closer to the spectators in terms of physical capabilities, there are fewer distractions, and you can get close enough to the action to really watch what is happening. If you are interested enough to observe matches and have enough time to do so, watch the papers for announcements of tournaments and matches to be played in your area.

WATCHING FOR PREPARATION

Once you decide to try to learn by watching, what should you watch for? First, look for the way strokes are produced by the players. Start with their preparation for shots. Most spectators cannot resist the temptation to watch the ball first and everything else if they get a chance; watch what good players do *after* they hit shots, though.

- How do they get ready for the next shot?
- Where do they move on the court?
- What parts of the court do they protect or leave unprotected?
- How do they move their feet in preparing for shots?
- How many steps do they take to get from the baseline to a volleying position?
- How long does it take them to get to that position?
- When and where do they plant their feet prior to a shot?
- In which direction do they turn the upper part of their body?

- Do they move toward the ball in a direct line?
- Where is the racket head while they are moving to hit a shot?

WATCHING TO SEE HOW STROKES ARE PRODUCED

After spending some time concentrating on the players' preparation, try to answer these questions about the strokes they are hitting:

- Where is the racket head in relation to the waist of the hitters when contact is made? Is it below, above, or even with the belt?
- Where do the players make contact with the ball? Is it in front of, even with, or behind the body?
- Are shots hit with backspin, topspin, sidespin, or no spin?
- Do the players you are watching swing from the shoulder or the elbow?
- Do they use the wrist (does it flex or extend) on some shots? Which ones?
- How do they transfer their weight as they hit?
- How high over the net do their groundstrokes travel?
- On serves, how high do they toss the ball?
- At what point is contact made on serves?
- What kind of spin is put on the serves?
- Is there a difference between the first and second serves?
- What is the difference?
- How close to the net do the players stand for volleys?
- How much of a backswing do they take?
- Do they crouch to hit some shots? Which ones?
- Where is contact made on volleys?
- Do they use a full swing or restricted swing on smashes?

WATCHING FOR STRATEGY

When you are tired of looking for little things in the strokes, think about match strategy for a while. Try to figure out what the players are thinking about when they use their strokes.

- Are shots being placed to particular spots on the court?
- Does the player who is winning use different strategy than the one losing?
- Does each player have a game plan? What is it?
- Does one player get to the net more often than the other?
- Is there one shot that produces repeated winners for either player?
- If you were the player losing the match, what would you do differently?
- Are the players using percentage shots or do they gamble with high-risk shots?
- Which, if any, shots are used more in doubles than in singles?
- Where do doubles partners line up to begin points?

PUTTING INFORMATION TO USE

The ultimate test of how well you have observed a match is to be able to answer many of the previous questions about a specific player *after* the match has been played. Do you just know who won and remember a few good shots, or can you tell someone else exactly how a player executed the shots and used a plan of attack?

Even if you can remember the details of some players' styles and approaches to the game, it will not do you any good unless you can incorporate some of their strengths into parts of your game that are weak. Don't try to take in so much of someone else's game that you become confused or simply imitate a style for no reason. Find the player who can do something well that you cannot do effectively or consistently, and copy the way he or she does it.

You must be able to imitate the movement of others to play tennis well. People are not born with an innate knowledge of how to hit a tennis ball correctly. The good athlete can watch someone execute a series of physical movements and come very close to imitating those movements. The lesser athlete must work to make his or her body do what some people can do almost naturally. So when you observe that stroke that looks right to you, capture the total picture in your mind, then transfer the picture from your mind to your body.

SCOUTING AN OPPONENT

If you watch a tennis match in order to scout a future opponent, you should be looking for other things. Your objective now is to learn how to beat this player. You will have a better chance of winning if you can answer some of the following questions about the player's game and then do something in your match to take advantage of the information you have gathered.

- Who is the player?
- Who is the opponent?
- Who won?
- What was the score?
- What kind of surface was the match played on?
- Is the player right-handed or left-handed?
- In one or two words, how would you describe this player's forehand, backhand, serve, forehand volley, backhand volley, and overhead smash?
- Where is the first serve usually placed? Second serve?
- Where should you stand to receive serves?
- What is this player's best shot?
- What can you do to prevent this player from hitting that shot?
- What is the weakest shot?
- What can you do to make this player hit that weakest shot?
- Does the player have any unusual shot?
- Is there a preference to play in the backcourt or at the net?
- On which shots does this player go to the net?
- What percentage of smashes are hit into the court?
- Can these smashes be retrieved?
- Does the player have a good lob?
- How many first serves are gotten in during a game?
- Is the player in good physical condition?
- Is the player fast or slow?
- Is the ball kept in play for long rallies?
- Is the player honest on calls?
- Does the player concentrate fully, or does his or her mind wander?
- Is the player as composed when behind as when ahead in the match?
- What are two things you will have to do to win a match against this player?

If you have all of this information about an opponent, you will be better prepared to plan the match than 99% of all the tennis players in the world. Most people do not have the time to get that kind of report on a player before a match. If you do not have the time, consider writing down what you learn about an opponent after you have played the match. You may play each other again.

Remember that no matter how much you know about another player and no matter how well you plan your strategy, you have to be able to consistently keep the ball in play for your strategy to work. Until you reach a level where you can do that, you are not ready for scouting other players. Use the Postmatch Scouting Form to make notes on a completed match.

CHARTING YOUR MATCHES

In order to learn exactly what your strengths and weaknesses are, have a friend or classmate chart one of your matches. *Charting* means recording how points are won or lost. In some cases, what you perceive to be happening during a match and what is actually happening are not the same. In the heat of a match, a few good or bad shots may stand out in your mind even though more subtle facets of your game may determine whether you win or lose. Although there are elaborate, computerized systems of charting used by coaches and tournament players, there are simple ways to keep track of what is happening. Use the Error Chart and the Winning Shot Chart to chart your next match.

Postmatch Scouting Form

Directions: Play a set or a match, then complete this form.

Name of opponent _____ Date of match _____

Results of match: _____ Won, _____ Lost; Score _____

Type of court _____ Weather _____

WRITE ONE OBSERVATION IN EACH CATEGORY ABOUT YOUR OPPONENT

Forehand _____

Backhand _____

First serve _____

Second serve _____

Forehand volley _____

Backhand volley _____

Smash _____

Best shot _____

Weakest shot _____

Speed _____

Strength _____

Quickness _____

Endurance _____

Style of play _____

Right-handed/left-handed _____

Honesty on calls _____

Comments _____

Error Chart

Directions: Tally errors made in each game on the strokes listed in the left column. For example, if the first serve fails to go into the proper court three times in the first game, mark "III" in that box.

Game

Stroke	1	2	3	4	5	6	7	8	9
1st serve									
2nd serve									
FH serve return									
BH serve return									
FH groundstroke									
BH groundstroke									
Forehand volley									
Backhand volley									
Lob									
Smash									
Drop shot									

Winning Shot Chart

Directions: Tally winning shots during each game for the strokes listed in the left column.

Game

Stroke	1	2	3	4	5	6	7	8	9
1st serve									
2nd serve									
FH serve return									
BH serve return									
FH groundstroke									
BH groundstroke									
Forehand volley									
Backhand volley									
Lob									
Smash									
Drop shot									

As with any other physical activity, it is possible to get hurt playing tennis. Although tennis elbow gets most of the publicity, there are several less serious, but more common, injuries among tennis players. Blisters, sprains, strains, cramps, and shin splints, as well as tennis elbow, are examples of problems almost all players encounter sooner or later. In most cases, tennis injuries are not emergencies, so the player who has some information about them can take care of him- or herself.

BLISTERS

Beginners and people who have not played for a while are probably going to get blisters on the racket hand and on the feet, in that order. A *blister* is an accumulation of fluid between the two top layers of the skin. Blisters are caused by irritation—in these cases, irritation between the racket and the hand, and between the foot and the sock, shoe, or court.

There are ways to reduce the possibility and frequency of blisters. Play for short periods of time when beginning a practice session; gradually increase the amount of playing time as your skin becomes tougher. Playing tennis for 2–3 hours the first day out is a sure way to develop blisters.

Make sure that the racket grip is the right size. Rackets with grips that are too large or too small tend to slip on impact, and this increases the amount of friction. Keep the racket handle as dry as possible. The more it slips, the more irritation to your hand occurs. Wear a tennis glove, or tape the areas of the hand most likely to blister. You may lose a degree of your sense of touch wearing a glove, but the glove can be removed after your hand toughens. In the meantime, cutting out the finger tips of the glove can restore the feel between hand and racket.

Avoid blisters on your feet by putting powder in your shoes or socks, wearing padded socks or two pairs of socks, and wearing shoes that fit.

If you get a blister and have to continue playing, clean the area with alcohol or soap and water, sterilize a needle (burn it with a lighted match), and make a very small opening at one edge of the affected area so the fluid can drain. Then place a bandage over the entire area. Some players can play with pain caused by blisters and others cannot.

Keep first aid supplies nearby, because the areas on the hands and feet likely to blister are difficult to bandage, and the bandages will come off as a result of movement and perspiration. Vaseline applications can reduce the friction, and there are products on the market that simulate the skin and cover the sore spot. In some cases, the top layer of skin can be removed, but this should only be done by a trainer or physician. Let the dead skin protect the layer underneath. If you do not have to play tennis for several days, leave the blister as it is. The fluid buildup is a natural protective reaction for the irritated skin. The skin will eventually heal, and the fluid will be reabsorbed if the area is protected long enough.

SPRAINS

A *sprain* is an injury to a joint that usually damages blood vessels, ligaments, and tendons. The injury is frequently caused by forcing a joint beyond the normal range of motion. In tennis, sprains most commonly occur in the ankles. The symptoms are swelling, tenderness, discoloration, and pain, especially upon movement or when weight is placed on the joint. An ankle can be sprained and fractured at the same time. The degree of pain should not be the only factor in trying to determine whether or not a break has occurred; sprains can hurt as much as breaks.

Remember *RICE* for first aid of sprains. The *R* is for *rest*. Don't be a hero or heroine and try to "walk it off" or resume play too soon. *I* is for *ice*—alternate 20 minutes on and 20 off during the first 48 hours after the injury. The purpose of cold is to reduce the flow of fluid into the area by constricting blood vessels. The *C* stands for *compression*—applying pressure to the affected part, also in order to control swelling. Compression is difficult unless you have the right supplies, but using towels, tape, and elastic bandages works. If not, you may need medical help. *E—elevate* the part of the body that has been sprained, in order to keep more fluid from increasing the swelling. Sprained joints can be more susceptible to subsequent sprains, so tape the joint for support when you are ready to play again, even if it feels fine.

STRAINS

Strains are tears in muscle and connective tissue. They are also called *pulled muscles* and *muscle tears*. They can be caused by over-exercising, sudden movement, fatigue, and not warming up properly. Pulled muscles in the legs, back, and wrist are common among tennis players. The symptoms are pain when the muscles are exercised, general soreness, and muscle spasms. Most trainers now use the method of alternately applying ice packs 20 minutes on and 20 minutes off for the first day after a muscle has been injured. If you continue to play, using heat to increase circulation may help before competition, and ice is helpful immediately after playing.

Trainers, therapists, and physicians can treat pulled muscles with more sophisticated methods such as ultrasound, medication, and electrical stimulation. If your injury is serious enough, get help from a specialist.

CRAMPS

Cramps are involuntary contractions of muscles and can be caused by many things. Fatigue, overexertion, and chemical imbalances seem to trigger cramps in tennis players. Conditioning programs could eliminate some of the cramps caused by fatigue and overexertion. Electrolyte imbalance can be avoided by maintaining a balance between potassium, sodium,

and water. The idea is to replace all three substances in proper proportions during and after competition. Loading up with salt immediately before a match won't help; eating a banana or two might.

Pressure on the cramped area, stretching the muscle, ice applications, and massages are used in giving first aid. Muscles where spasms occur might cramp up again, so be careful when you decide to resume playing.

SHIN SPLINTS

A *shin splint* is a rather vague term referring to pain in the front part of the lower leg. There are a lot of things that could go wrong down there, but it is safe to say that shin splints involve inflammation of tendons and muscles in that area of the leg. They can be caused by running on hard surfaces, poor conditioning, poor running technique, or congenital problems. Poor arch supports can also cause or compound the problem.

Tennis players are more likely to develop shin splints after a long layoff, especially if they play on hard courts. The treatment involves taping and elevating the arch, playing in well-made shoes, resting, and applying ice. Fill a paper cup with water, freeze it, and rub the shin splint area with ice 10 minutes at a time, several times a day. This may help reduce the inflammation.

Try to avoid shin splints by sound conditioning, practicing in sessions that increase gradually from short to longer periods of time, and playing on cushioned surfaces.

TENNIS ELBOW

Tennis elbow affects about one third of all regular tennis players sooner or later. It is probably the most studied and researched of all tennis injuries, yet there are still as many questions as there are answers about the problem.

Tennis elbow is an inflammation of the tissues, especially the tendons, around the end of the bone in the upper arm at the elbow. *Tendinitis* is a more accurate medical term for the condition. Bone fragments can cause the pain, as can the constant impact of the ball on the racket (producing stress in the forearm muscles), improper hitting technique, weak muscles, and using a racket not suited for you.

The primary symptom is severe pain in the elbow—most of the time on the outside (lateral), but occasionally on the inside (medial), part of the arm. This pain may occur only on certain shots or in certain positions of the arm, but if the injury is serious enough, there could be pain to the touch, when you shake hands, or even when you brush your teeth.

No single method of treatment is effective for everyone, so see a doctor, physical therapist, or trainer if it is a serious problem. If not, try ice packs for 20 minutes, 2 or 3 times a day. Aspirin or ibuprofen may relieve the pain temporarily, and rest is a more permanent alternative. Elbow braces and constricting bands around the forearm work for some people. Changing rackets can help if the new racket either absorbs more of the pressure or shifts it to another part of the arm.

SUMMARY OF TENNIS INJURIES, CAUSES, AND TREATMENTS

Injury	Causes	Treatment
Blisters	• Racket hand irritation • Foot, sock, shoe irritation	• Clean area • Open area to drain • Skin lube • Bandage and tape
Sprains	• Forcing joints beyond normal range of motion	• Ice for 24–48 hours • Compression • Elevation • Rest
Strains	• Overexertion • Sudden movement • Fatigue • Improper warm-up	• Ice every 20 minutes during first day after injury • Heat before playing • Ice after playing
Cramps	• Fatigue • Overexertion • Chemical imbalance	• Stretching affected muscle • Ice • Massage • Pressure
Shin splints	• Hard surfaces • Poor conditioning • Inadequate arch support • Poor running technique • Congenital problems	• Taping or elevating arch • Proper shoes • Ice • Rest
Tennis elbow	• Forearm stress • Weak muscles • Improper hitting technique • Wrong racket • Bone fragments	• Ice • Aspirin or ibuprofen • Rest • Different racket • Arm bands

Rating Your Total Progress

Rate your success so far in tennis by writing a number in one of the five spaces provided to the right of each tennis skill listed. Then total the numbers when you finish. The higher the score, the better.

Rating Points	1 Unsuccessful	2 Below average	3 Average success	4 Above average	5 Very successful
Handling the racket	_____	_____	_____	_____	_____
Preparing to hit	_____	_____	_____	_____	_____
Forehand	_____	_____	_____	_____	_____
Backhand	_____	_____	_____	_____	_____
Groundstroke combinations	_____	_____	_____	_____	_____
Beginner's punch serve	_____	_____	_____	_____	_____
Full swing serve	_____	_____	_____	_____	_____
3-shot singles	_____	_____	_____	_____	_____
Beginner's volley	_____	_____	_____	_____	_____
Lob	_____	_____	_____	_____	_____
Smash	_____	_____	_____	_____	_____
Volley-lob-smash combinations	_____	_____	_____	_____	_____
Advanced volley	_____	_____	_____	_____	_____
Half volley	_____	_____	_____	_____	_____
Drop shot	_____	_____	_____	_____	_____
Keeping score	_____	_____	_____	_____	_____
Understanding singles strategy	_____	_____	_____	_____	_____
Understanding doubles strategy	_____	_____	_____	_____	_____
Limiting self-talk	_____	_____	_____	_____	_____
Ability to block out noise	_____	_____	_____	_____	_____
Persistence	_____	_____	_____	_____	_____
Ability to come from behind	_____	_____	_____	_____	_____
Point planning	_____	_____	_____	_____	_____
Goal setting	_____	_____	_____	_____	_____
Ability to learn by watching	_____	_____	_____	_____	_____
Subtotal =	_____	_____	_____	_____	_____

Total score = _____

186 Tennis: Steps to Success

Compare your total score with the following rating point scale to get a general indication of your skills:

- a perfect self-rating is 125 points
- an above average score ranges from 100 to 124 points
- an average score ranges from 65 to 99 points
- a below average score ranges from 50 to 64 points

Now look back at your self-ratings for each tennis skill. What does this tell you about your areas of strengths and weaknesses? What goals would you prepare for yourself to increase your tennis skills and future enjoyment?

Appendix

Individual Program

INDIVIDUAL COURSE IN _____   GRADE/COURSE SECTION _____

STUDENT'S NAME _____   STUDENT ID # _____

SKILLS/CONCEPTS	TECHNIQUE AND PERFORMANCE OBJECTIVES	WT* ×	POINT PROGRESS** =				FINAL SCORE***
			1	2	3	4	

Note. From "The Role of Expert Knowledge Structures in an Instructional Design Model for Physical Education" by J.N. Vickers, 1983, *Journal of Teaching in Physical Education,* **2**(3), p. 17. Copyright 1983 by Joan N. Vickers. Adapted by permission.

*WT = Weighting of an objective's degree of difficulty.

**PROGRESS = Ongoing success, which may be expressed in terms of (a) accumulated points (1, 2, 3, 4); (b) grades (D, C, B, A); (c) symbols (merit, bronze, silver, gold); (d) unsatisfactory/satisfactory; and others as desired.

***FINAL SCORE equals WT times PROGRESS.

ace A service winner that the receiver cannot touch with the racket.

ad Advantage; refers to the point after the score is deuce.

ad court The left half of a player's court as that player faces the net from the baseline.

ad in A reference to the score when the player serving has won the point after the score was deuce.

ad out A reference to the score when the player receiving the serve has won the point after the score was deuce.

all A tie score; *30-all*, for example, means that the score is 30–30.

alley A lane, 4½-foot–wide, running parallel to, and on both sides of, the singles court. The alleys are in play for all shots after the serve in doubles.

amateur A person who does not accept money for playing or teaching tennis.

American twist A type of serve in which the spin imparted by the racket is the opposite of what it would be normally. A right-hander's American twist serve puts left-to-right spin on the ball.

angle shot A shot that crosses the net at a severe angle.

approach shot A shot that the hitter follows to the net.

Association of Tennis Professionals (ATP) An organization composed of most of the leading male players in the world.

Australian doubles A doubles formation in which the player at the net (the server's partner) lines up on the same half of the doubles court as the server.

backcourt The part of the court between the service line and the baseline.

backhand A stroke that a right-handed player hits by reaching across the body to the left side; a left-handed player reaches across to the right side to hit a backhand.

backspin Reverse spin on the ball, like a car wheel in reverse.

backswing The preparation for a stroke in which the racket is drawn back before being swung forward.

balance point The point in the shaft of a racket where the head and the handle are balanced.

baseline The boundary line that runs parallel to, and 39 feet from, the net.

block The return of a ball with a very short swinging motion.

boron An extremely strong, stiff, light metalloid element used to make some tennis rackets.

breaking serve The loss of a game by the player serving.

carry A shot that is carried on the racket strings, slung, or hit twice as the ball is returned. Carries are legal unless the player makes two or more deliberate attempts to hit the ball over the net; carries may be called by the umpire or by the player who hits the ball.

center mark A line dividing the baseline at the center. The server may not legally step on the center mark before striking the ball.

center service line The line in the middle of the court that divides the two service courts.

ceramic Very strong and durable material used in some rackets.

chip A groundstroke hit with a short backswing and with backspin on the ball. The chip is usually meant to be a shallow shot (not very deep into the opponent's court).

choke To play poorly because of the pressure of competition.

choke up To hold the racket at a point higher up the handle, away from the base of the grip.

chop A shot hit with backspin to any part of the court.

circuit A series of tournaments at the state, sectional, national, or international level.

closed stance A position in which the toes of both feet form a line parallel to either sideline.

closed tournament An event open only to players in a particular geographical area.

composite A reference to tennis rackets made from a combination of two or more materials; for example, graphite and ceramics.

Continental grip A way of holding the racket so that the player does not have to change grips between the forehand and backhand strokes; the wrist is directly over the top of the grip.

cross-strings Strings running horizontally from one side of the racket head to the other.

crosscourt A shot hit diagonally from one corner of the court to the opposite corner.

Davis Cup An international team tennis event for male players.

deep A reference to the area near the baseline.

default The awarding of a match to one player or team because an opponent fails to appear or is not able to complete a match; synonym for forfeit.

deuce A tie score at 40–40, and each tie thereafter in the same game.

deuce court The right half of a player's court as that player faces the baseline.

dink A shot hit with very little pace or depth.

double fault Failure on both attempts to serve into the proper court.

doubles A match played with four players. Also, an informal expression sometimes used to indicate a double fault.

down-the-line shot A shot hit more or less parallel to the closer sideline.

drive A groundstroke hit forcefully and deeply into an opponent's backcourt.

drop shot A softly hit shot, usually having backspin, that barely clears the net and bounces twice before the opponent can get to it.

Eastern backhand grip A grip in which the V formed by the thumb and index finger is above but slightly toward the left of the racket handle as a right-handed player prepares to hit a backhand.

Eastern forehand grip A grip in which the V formed by the thumb and index finger is above but slightly toward the right of the racket handle as a right-handed player prepares to hit a forehand.

error A point lost as a result of one player's mistake rather than the other player's good shot.

face The flat hitting surface formed by the strings and the racket head.

fast A reference to a tennis court surface on which the ball bounces low and moves rapidly toward or away from the hitter.

fault Failure on an attempt to serve into the proper court.

Federation Cup An international team tennis event for female players.

feed-in consolation A tournament in which players who lose in the early rounds of a tournament reenter the championship draw and may finish as high as fifth.

fiberglass A somewhat flexible form of glass fiber material used in some rackets.

finals The match played in a tournament to determine the winner of a tournament.

flat A reference to a shot hit with little or no spin. Also a term used to describe tennis balls that have lost their firmness and resilience.

flexibility How much a racket bends from head to shaft or from one side of the head to the other when contact with the ball is made.

follow-through The part of the swinging motion after the ball has been hit.

forehand A stroke that a right-handed player hits on the right side of the body and a left-hander hits on the left side.

forfeit The awarding of a match to one player or team because an opponent fails to appear or is not able to complete a match; synonym for *default*.

frame The tennis racket, excluding the strings.

graphite A man-made, carbon-based material 20 times stronger and stiffer than wood, often used in rackets.

grip The manner in which a racket is held. Also, the part of the racket where it is held.

grommet A small, round plastic sleeve in the frame, through which the strings pass.

groove To hit shots in a patterned, disciplined, and consistent manner.

groundstroke A shot that is hit with a forehand or backhand stroke after the ball has bounced on the court.

gut Racket string made from animal intestines.

hacker A person who does not play tennis well.

half volley A shot hit just after the ball has bounced on the court; contact is made below the level of the knees.

head The upper part of the racket, where the strings are attached.

head-heavy A reference to a racket whose balance point is more than $1/4$ inch from the center (midpoint of the racket's length) toward the head.

head-light A reference to a racket whose balance point is more than $1/4$ inch from the center (midpoint of the racket's length) toward the handle.

hitting surface The flat surface formed by the strings.

holding serve The server winning the game.

hook A slang term meaning to cheat.

International Tennis Federation (ITF) An organization that governs international amateur competition and that has some jurisdiction over professional tennis.

invitational tournament A tournament open only to players who have been invited to participate.

junior A player 18 years old or younger.

Kevlar A synthetic fiber used to strengthen tennis racket frames.

ladder tournament A type of competition in which the names of participants are placed in a column; players can advance up the column (ladder) by challenging and defeating players whose names appear above their own.

let A serve that hits the top of the net and bounces in the proper service court. Also, an expression used to indicate that a point should be replayed for one of a number of other reasons.

linesperson An official who is responsible for calling shots either in or out at either the baseline, service line, sideline, or center service line.

lob A high, arching shot.

lob volley A lob hit with a volley.

long An informal expression used to indicate that a shot went out past the baseline.

love An archaic but commonly used way to say *zero* in the tennis scoring system.

main strings The vertical strings, running from the top of the racket head to its bottom.

match Competition between two players in singles, four players in doubles, or between two teams, as when two school teams compete against each other.

match point The stage of a match when a player or team can win the match by winning the next point. The term is used by spectators and television announcers during a match and by players after a match; it is not, or should not be, used by the umpire or players in calling out the score.

mixed doubles Competition pairing a man and woman on one team against a man and woman on the other team.

net umpire The official who is responsible for calling let serves.

no An informal expression used by some players to call shots out.

no-ad   A scoring system in which a maximum of 7 points constitutes a game. For example, if the score is tied at 3 points for each player, the next player to win a point wins the game.

not up   An expression used to indicate that a ball has bounced twice on the same side before being hit.

no-man's-land   The area of the court between the service line and the baseline. This area is usually considered a weak area from which to return shots during a rally.

nylon   A strong, synthetic stringing material.

open tennis   Competition open to amateur and professional players.

out   A call indicating that a shot has bounced outside a boundary line.

overhead smash   A hard, powerful stroke hit from an over-the-head racket position.

pace   The velocity with which a ball is hit.

passing shot   A groundstroke hit out of the reach of an opponent at the net.

percentage shot   The safest, most effective shot hit in a particular situation.

placement   A winning shot hit to an open area of the court.

poaching   A doubles player at the net cutting in front of the partner to hit a volley.

point penalty   A system in which a player may be penalized points, games, or even matches for improper conduct.

power zone   The area of the racket's hitting surface that produces controlled power with no vibration.

pro set   A match that is completed when one player or team has won at least 8 games and is ahead by at least 2 games.

pusher   A type of player who is consistent, but who hits with very little pace.

put-away   A shot that is literally put away (out of reach) from an opponent.

qualifying round   A series of matches played to determine which players will be added to a tournament field.

rally   An exchange of shots.

ready position   The position in which a player stands while waiting for a shot.

receiver   The player who returns a serve.

referee   The official who is responsible for supervising all competition during a tournament.

retriever   A type of player, much like the pusher, who gets everything back but does not play aggressively.

round-robin   A type of competition in which all participants compete against all other participants in a series of matches. The player or team finishing the competition with the best win-loss percentage is the winner.

rush   To move toward the net following a forcing shot.

second   An informal expression used by some players to indicate that the first serve was out.

serve   The shot used to put the ball into play at the beginning of a point.

service break   The loss of a game by the player serving.

service court   The area into which the ball must be served; its boundaries are the net, the center line, the service line, and the singles sideline.

service line   The line that is parallel to, and 21 feet from, the net.

set   The part of a match that is completed when a player or team has won at least 6 games and is ahead by at least 2 games.

set point   The stage of a set when a player or team can win the set by winning the next point.

shaft   The part of the racket between the head and the grip.

sideline   The boundary that runs from the net to the baseline; the singles sidelines are closer to the center of the court than the doubles sidelines.

single elimination tournament   A type of competition in which players' names are drawn and placed on lines in a tournament bracket; matches are played between players whose names appear on connected bracket lines. Players who win advance to the next round of competition; those who lose a match are eliminated.

slice   To hit a ball with sidespin, like the spin of a top.

slow   A description of a court surface on which the ball slows down after the bounce.

split sets   An expression used to indicate that the two opposing players or teams have each won a set.

straight sets   A reference to winning a match without losing a set.

stroke   The manner in which a player hits the ball (forehand, backhand, volley, etc.).

sweet spot   The exact place on the racket face that produces controlled power with no vibration.

synthetics   A type of string made from specially designed nylon.

take two   An expression meaning that the server should repeat both service attempts.

teaching pro   A person who teaches people to play tennis and is paid for the service. Teaching pros are usually distinguished from playing pros, although some professionals teach and play for money.

throat   The part of the racket just below the head; the yoke.

tiebreaker   A method of completing a set when both players or teams have won 6 games.

titanium   A strong, lustrous, white metallic element used to make some rackets.

topspin   The bottom-to-top rotation imparted to a ball by the racket, like a car wheel going forward.

touch   The ability to hit a variety of controlled, precision shots.

umpire   The person who is responsible for officiating a match between two players or teams.

unforced error   A point lost with absolutely no pressure having been exerted by the opponent.

United States Tennis Association (USTA)   A national, noncommercial membership organization that promotes tennis in a variety of ways.

volley   A shot hit before the ball bounces on the court.

Western grip   A way of holding the racket in which the wrist is positioned directly behind the handle.

wide   An expression used by some players to indicate a shot went out beyond a sideline.

Wimbledon   A tennis tournament in England, generally considered to be the most prestigious in the world.

Women's International Tennis Association (WITA)   An organization consisting of the world's leading female professional players.

yoke   The part of the racket immediately below the head; the upper part of the shaft; the throat.

About the Author

Jim Brown is a professor of health and physical education at McNeese University in Lake Charles, Louisiana. He began playing tennis more than 35 years ago and has experience as a teaching professional, a college instructor and coach, a city program director, a writer and publisher, a consultant, and a clinician. He has written, coauthored, or edited 8 books and more than 50 articles on a variety of health and physical education topics. Dr. Brown has represented the United States Tennis Association, the American Alliance for Health, Physical Education, Recreation and Dance, and the President's Council on Physical Fitness and Sports in clinics throughout the United States and Mexico. In addition to his teaching duties at McNeese, he is the director of the McNeese Community Tennis Program and a member of the Wilson Sporting Goods tennis advisory staff.